ONE HUNDRED ONE
Upward
Glances

Watching for God's Touch in the Ordinary Days

Sandra P. Aldrich

Tyndale House Publishers, Inc.
WHEATON, ILLINOIS

To two people for whom I am most grateful:

my daughter-in-law, Marianne Reddin Aldrich,

and my son-in-law, Eric Boyd Hulen.

Visit Tyndale's exciting Web site at www.tyndale.com

Copyright © 2000 by Sandra Picklesimer Aldrich. All rights reserved.

Illustrations copyright © 2000 by Donna Kae Nelson. All rights reserved.

Designed by Melinda Schumacher

Published in association with the literary agency of Alive Communications, Inc., 7680 Goddard Street, Suite 200, Colorado Springs, CO 80920.

Library of Congress Cataloging-in-Publication Data

Aldrich, Sandra Picklesimer.
   One hundred one upward glances : watching for God's touch in the ordinary days / Sandra Picklesimer Aldrich.
   p. cm.
   ISBN 0-8423-3604-4
   1. Christian women—Religious life. 2. Aldrich, Sandra Picklesimer. I. Title: One hundred and one upward glances. II. Title.

BV4527 .A43 2000
242—dc21

00-039300

Printed in the United States of America

06 05 04 03 02 01 00
7 6 5 4 3 2 1

Contents

The Joy of the Lord

A Patchwork of Wisdom

Workdays, Holidays, and Every Days

Courage

Dear Reader,

If you've picked up this book hoping to hear from a "proper Christian woman" who knows exactly how to live a perfect life, then please close the cover right now and meander over to the fiction section of the store. But if you're interested in reading about an imperfect woman who loves her perfect Savior, then you're welcome to hang around.

The 101 glances you are holding are part of my personal journey in this great adventure of learning more about the Lord—and more about myself. Many of these experiences have been so significant in my spiritual growth that I've shared them with my audiences. Some are included in previous books. Several were retold over the four years I wrote and recorded "A Single Moment" for the Focus on the Family Weekend broadcast. So, sit back and (I hope) enjoy these little anecdotes as you ponder how God is working in your life, too. But always be aware that the Lord is real—we do not pray to air—and he waits to be invited into every detail of our lives.

I've found that the Lord's encouragement often comes through the people around us, and this project has been no exception. I want to express warmest appreciation for the folks at Alive Communications, Inc., especially my literary agent, Greg Johnson, and to the Focus on the Family/Tyndale House Publishing teams—especially Jan Long Harris. Thanks to all of you for agreeing yet again to work with this feisty Kentucky woman. God bless!

Sandra Picklesimer Aldrich
Colorado Springs, Colorado

THE POWER OF
ENCOURAGEMENT

"You Good Mama"

But encourage one another daily,
as long as it is called Today.
HEBREWS 3:13

W e all have those moments when we're so tired and
discouraged that we don't think we can take another step.
Several years ago, though, three simple words from a fellow
traveler proved to be God's special encouragement to me
during one of those times. My then-young children and I
were on a church tour in Italy, sharing a bus with a group
visiting from Mexico City. We couldn't communicate with the
Spanish-speaking travelers, but we smiled and nodded at each
other as our separate guides explained the various historical
sights.

For Jay, Holly, and me, the trip was supposed to be a
reward for our perseverance in adjusting to being a family
of three after my husband, Don, died from brain cancer. But
instead, the tour proved to be overwhelming. The first day,
I had briefly lost twelve-year-old Jay twice, was soundly
cheated in the purchase of a souvenir, and was constantly
reminded by the sight of numerous couples that I was single
and raising my children *alone.*

By the time we stopped for dinner, I was thinking I'd made

a mistake in taking the trip. How was I going to raise two children alone when I couldn't even keep track of them for a day?

As we lined up for the washroom, one of the men in our group put his hand on Jay's shoulder, making sure he didn't stray. I rested my arms on top of Holly's head as she leaned against me. I was tired and feeling defeated.

Then one of the Mexican grandmothers stopped in front of me, patted my arm, and said haltingly, "You good mama."

Three simple words, certainly, but they carried incredible power. Suddenly I wasn't so exhausted, and my fear was replaced with the hope that maybe, just maybe, I could pull this single-parenting thing off after all.

The grandmother's kind words had injected me with strength. And in that moment she became for me God's reminder he hadn't forgotten me, that I could—with his help—get through the challenges of raising two young children alone.

We all can offer similar verbal pats on the back. Look around. You won't have to search very far for folks who need your smile and the reminder that despite the struggle, they are doing a good job.

To Ponder:

Describe a time when you felt overwhelmed.

Did anyone encourage you during this time? If so, how? If not, why do you think no one stepped forward?

How do you try to encourage others in their struggles?

So You Think You Don't Make a Difference?

I thank my God every time I remember you.
PHILIPPIANS 1:3

A while back, I was in one of those woe-is-me moods in which you feel as though you'll never make a difference in this pitiful world. Out of habit, I picked up my old white Bible, the one from my junior high school days, and flipped through its pages, looking for wisdom. I found it quickly, but not where I had expected. For on one of the back pages was the long-ago autograph of Mitsuo Fuchida, a speaker I had heard at a youth rally during my senior year. He told of returning to Japan embittered because not one American family had invited him into their home during his four long, lonely years as a student here in the States. When his nation later asked him to lead the attack on Pearl Harbor, he accepted gladly and without hesitation. It was only after the war was over that he met a Christian who befriended him and introduced him to Jesus.

Then I remembered the account a former Ethiopian senator had given about Mangusto, a young African who had encountered only prejudice as a student in the United States during the late 1960s. When Mangusto came into power in his own country, he expelled missionaries and welcomed the Marxists, who would eventually take over in Ethiopia, one of the world's oldest Christian nations.

As I reflected on the difference *one* friend might have made in both of those cases, I reminded myself that while my kindness probably won't stop a world war or keep governments from toppling, it can make a difference in another person's life. And we never know how a sincere compliment, a bit of encouragement, or even an invitation to dinner will play itself out—within a home or within a nation.

So I picked up the phone and invited a recent widow to accompany me to my favorite tea shop. Suddenly my day was no longer bleak. And who knows? Maybe I made a difference in someone's world after all.

To Ponder:

Has anyone offered you friendship when you were lonely?
What opportunities do you have to extend hospitality to others?
What sensitivities do you think are needed to make reaching out work?

But That's Not Fair!

He causes his sun to rise on the evil and the good, and sends
rain on the righteous and the unrighteous.
MATTHEW 5:45

When I was growing up, I tried not to grump, "But that's
not fair!" around my grandmother, Mama Farley. If she
caught me saying it, she always gently replied, "Honey, there
are some things in life that all you can do with 'em is bear
'em."

But I never wanted to bear any injustice; I wanted the situation corrected. For example, I remember one ancient relative
who told stories about our family's involvement in the War
between the States, as she called it. She said the men in our
secluded area had gone to the battlefields, leaving their wives
and children alone on the Kentucky hillside farms.

On the home front, first one army, then the other, had
stolen everything they could, including her family's lone milk
cow. But late one afternoon horsemen stormed into the yard,
demanding the last of their food. Her feisty mother started to
argue, saying her "young'uns" needed it. Unswayed, the
leader pointed his pistol and said it would be a shame to have
to shoot her in front of the children. She gave the soldiers the
food.

Over the years, the story was retold so much and became so real to me I could have reported the color of the leader's hair. But as I'd express my indignation, Mama Farley would say again, "Remember, honey, there are some things in life that all you can do with 'em is bear 'em. And you bear them best by hanging on to the Lord."

In this century, our family hasn't had to give up the last of the food, and we haven't had a war fought on our property. But we all still face challenges, and we're still learning the truth of Mama Farley's patient encouragement to bear life's troubles with the Lord's help. After all, that's the best way—sometimes the *only* way—to get through the day.

To Ponder:

When are you prone to say, "It's not fair"?

Did anyone in your youth try to help you understand life's unfairness?

Has anyone in your family ever questioned God because of a perceived injustice? What did you say or do to help?

Just like Doris!

In everything set them an example by doing what is good.
In your teaching show integrity, seriousness.
TITUS 2:7

What would happen if we fully understood the power of encouragement to change a life? I've witnessed that power in my own life. In fact, a few kind words when I was only twelve gave me the vision to get an education. The summer before I entered seventh grade, I met Doris Schumacher, a teacher visiting her elderly Aunt Minnie, who lived across the street from my family.

Schoolteachers frightened me because several of mine had ridiculed my Kentucky speech patterns, so I was immediately intimidated by Doris, too.

But she smiled and said, "Aunt Minnie tells me you're going into junior high this fall. Tell me, what do you like to study?"

I was surprised by her question. I usually heard only "How's school?" from adults.

I managed, "Well, I like to read, and I like history."

She smiled again, and her graying hair seemed like a halo. "That's wonderful," she said. "I teach eighth-grade English and social studies in Minneapolis. What do you like to read?"

Two direct questions from an adult! Stammering, I told her about the books I had read that past week.

She nodded approvingly. "Good choices," she said. Then her aunt came into the room with an errand list, and I turned to leave. But Doris added, "I assume you're nervous about going into junior high. Don't be; you'll do just fine!"

The conversation had probably taken all of three minutes, but by the time I walked across the street and up our front steps, I was determined to be a teacher "just like Doris!"

It was the 1950s and none of the women in my extended family had attended college, so my announcement was a bit unsettling to some of the relatives. But I pulled that dream into my heart and, with God's grace and my perseverance, gained the bachelor of arts and master of fine arts degrees that gave me fifteen years in a Detroit-area classroom. Later, those same degrees opened the door for me to pursue an editing career and rebuild my life after my husband died.

Doris is in her late nineties now, but she has continued to encourage me over the decades. One snowy morning years ago, as we chatted over long-distance lines, she commented about how far I had come since my school days.

"You're a big part of that success," I said. "You gave me the vision to go to college." Then I began to tell her about our long-ago, three-minute meeting.

She interrupted me. "No, dear," she said. "The first time I met you was when you were fifteen and visiting Aunt Minnie at the hospital after she'd broken her hip."

"Oh, no, Doris," I insisted. "I was twelve. I remember you standing by the oak table in your Aunt Minnie's front room. I even remember the morning sun coming through the lace curtains, and your brown-and-gray sweater that matched your hair."

She sighed, then said, "Oh, my dear, I don't remember that morning at all."

I chuckled. "It's okay, Doris," I said. "It only changed my life!"

And truly her kindness had done exactly that.

To Ponder:

Has a simple remark ever had a profound influence on your life? What was it?

What do you wish someone had said to you when you were a child?

What types of encouraging things do you try to say to others?

How Do I Help a Hurting Friend?

Rejoice with those who rejoice;
mourn with those who mourn.
ROMANS 12:15

The call comes just after dinner. You barely recognize your friend's voice for the sobs. "There's been an accident. . . ." Or you have lunch with a coworker. Realizing that she seems unusually quiet, you ask if she's okay. "Well, no," she says. "My husband just walked out on me."

What do you say?

You know that the next few days will be a blur of explanations to the children, funeral arrangements, or lawyer appointments. Then will come the weeks of shattered dreams, painful adjustments to a new lifestyle, and grief for what has been lost. You grieve for your friend, and you want to help. But how?

I was fortunate enough to have several friends who knew how to help me during the confusing and frightening days right after my husband Don's death. They realized that grief, whether through death or divorce, is a process, and that while we may never get *over* sorrow, we can get *through* it. So they let me work through my churning emotions at my own pace. When I cried, they cried with me. When I laughed, they rejoiced and laughed, too. When I needed to talk—and talk—they listened.

Even those who had experienced their own great losses refrained from telling me how much worse their situations had been. They understood my need to grieve *my* loss. *And they didn't try to rush me toward healing.*

So, from the perspective of one who's been helped through a loss by caring friends, here's some advice: Be there for your friend when she needs you. She may need to talk, or she may need to cry, or she may just need a comforting presence. It may be tempting to tell your own painful stories, but remember that this is *her* grief.

Understand that anger is a normal response to pain. Your friend may well be angry with God, angry with her husband for walking out, or even angry with her husband for leaving her a widow too soon.

Encourage her, as my friends did, to be open with God and to bring all her tangled emotions to him. After all, God's shoulders are pretty big. He knows our heart anyway, so why shouldn't we talk to him honestly?

Then, offer practical help. Too often friends tell the grieving person, "Call if you need anything." But she may have so many needs she doesn't know where to begin. How much better if you offer to help in a specific way, such as "I'll be over Saturday morning to help you balance the checkbook."

And, always, keep praying for your friend. The old saying "Prayer may not change things, but it changes us for things" is true.

To Ponder:

What opportunities have you had to help a hurting friend?
How have you been helped during a difficult time?
How can you better help others? How can you let others know of your needs?

Take to Your Bed!

Why are you downcast, O my soul? Why so disturbed within
me? Put your hope in God, for I will yet praise him,
my Savior and my God.

PSALM 42:5-6

Jill, one of my former coworkers, had looked forward to
motherhood for years. But after the routine birth of her son,
she found herself depressed—much to her surprise and deep
disappointment. When I dropped off a gift for her baby, she
burst into tears, apologized for still being in her robe, then
added she didn't understand why she felt "so bummed" when
she had a wonderful husband and a darling newborn son.

I hadn't planned to stay for a visit, but I did exactly that.
After admiring her sleeping little boy, I made myself right at
home and prepared a cup of herbal tea for her. I urged her to
tell her doctor about the sadness at her next checkup, and
then we talked, woman to woman, about the changes her
body was going through after giving birth. I encouraged her
to eat nourishing foods, get as much rest as possible, stop
worrying about the condition of the house, and enjoy her
husband and new son.

Then I read Psalm 42:5 to let her know that her feelings
weren't "sin" but just part of the human experience. Even
though this portion of Scripture was written by King David

and not by a woman who had just given birth, it still speaks to our hurts today. This is the prayer of a believer who struggled with doubt and depression but finally came through the shadows to the place where he could again hope in God.

I told Jill that in my beloved Kentucky, we explain a person's temporary withdrawal from life with the nonjudgmental expression that she or he "took to bed"—to allow the body and spirit to heal during a period of solitude and time with God.

She suddenly looked hopeful. "You mean sometimes the most spiritual thing I can do is sleep?" she asked.

I grinned. "I believe it—especially when your body is recovering from a major event." Then I added, "I'm going to pray with you before I go, and then you're going to nap while your baby is asleep. Better days *are* ahead."

That scene took place a number of years ago, and Jill is now passing along the advice about "taking to bed" to other exhausted folks. I wish our culture would catch on to the concept that it's okay to rest and analyze our circumstances when we're feeling discouraged. Often when we're "cast down," it takes time before we can lift our faces again and jump into life's fray. Yes, the Lord is with us in all of our circumstances, but sometimes the best "weapon" we can take into our daily challenges is the clear head that comes from a well-rested body and spirit.

To Ponder:

Have you ever felt as though your soul was "cast down"?
   What was the circumstance?
What helps you when you feel discouraged?
What do you suggest to others who may be feeling overwhelmed by their circumstances?

Unexpected Encouragement

Forget the former things; do not dwell on the past.
See, I am doing a new thing!
ISAIAH 43:18-19

I remember one Michigan Saturday that wasn't going well at all. I was having trouble balancing the checkbook yet again, and my mechanic said the rocker arm—whatever that was—on the car had to be replaced.

I wanted to run away but settled for taking the three of us out for hamburgers. When we entered the restaurant, I saw that one of my former students—I'll call her Donna—was a waitress there.

Oh, good, I thought. *I'm tired and discouraged, and now I run into one of the most troublesome students I've had in fifteen years of teaching.* I could still see her in the front row of fifth-hour mythology class, arms folded and eyes daring me to make the lesson interesting.

Well, I wasn't going to disappoint Jay and Holly by going to another restaurant. I decided I'd just pretend I hadn't seen her. *Lord, just keep us from being seated in her section, please,* I prayed inwardly.

Where did the hostess lead us? Right to Donna's section, of course. *Anyplace but here,* I told myself. But just as I opened my mouth to ask for a booth near the window, Donna spotted us and came rushing over.

"Mrs. Aldrich! This is so neat!"

Sure, it'll be easier to poison me this way, I thought. But I managed a feeble smile.

"Guess what!" she said. "I'm a Christian now!"

I stood there dumbstruck as my mouth dropped open.

Donna just kept bubbling on. "My sister got saved at college," she said. "And it bugged me that she was always witnessing to me. Then I'd go to your class, and while we were studying the Greeks and Romans, you'd bring in something interesting from the Bible, and I'd get angry all over again.

"But I couldn't get what you both said out of my mind. And last year, I got saved! Isn't that neat?"

I was too choked up to talk, so I could only give her a hug. I realized that God had encouraged me by placing me exactly where I didn't want to be. And I marveled again at the work of the Holy Spirit—even when folks like me keep getting in the way.

To Ponder:

Has the Lord ever answered your prayer for encouragement in a way you weren't expecting—and really didn't want? What types of people do you least expect to encourage you? Has anyone who appeared to reject your witness later told you what your words meant?

Ready If Needed

*And my God will meet all your needs according
to his glorious riches in Christ Jesus.*
PHILIPPIANS 4:19

A friend was heading toward financial trouble–again. A
couple of raises at work had put me in a position to help, but
I didn't want her to look to me first. In the past I had gotten
caught in situations where folks expected me, the doer and
fixer, to rescue them from minor frustrations as well as major
challenges. Back then I had wondered if they ever prayed
before they picked up the phone, or if their immediate
thought was, *Call Sandra. She'll take care of this.*

So I wanted my friend to look to God as her Source, not to
me. But I also didn't want to deny help to someone in need.
As I thought of my friend's pattern of getting herself into
deep financial waters, I prayed for her and read Scripture
after Scripture, wondering if I should offer my help. Did my
faith mandate my rescuing her? I understood the single-
parent plight all too well, but I didn't want her to become
dependent on me. I wanted her to learn more about the Lord
and more about the strength he had given her. And, deep
down, I knew she needed financial counseling more than she
needed a loan.

One Sunday morning, those thoughts were heavy on my mind as I entered my usual row at church. In the quiet moments before the service began, I glanced around, taking mental roll call. The usual folks were in place, including my friends Larry and Mary Ellen Schaad. They were sitting behind the dear, elderly gentleman I'll call Mr. Smith, who was growing more feeble each week. But he had insisted he would continue to be in church as long as the Lord allowed. So each Sunday, we marveled at his determination to be independent—and held our breath each time he pulled himself to his feet.

On this particular morning, Mr. Smith seemed even more frail as he stood for a hymn. Then he wobbled as he backed toward his chair. Immediately, Larry Schaad's arms were at his shoulders, not touching him, but ready. Mr. Smith made it safely—and hadn't known Larry was ready to catch him if need be.

I let out the breath I was holding and realized I had just witnessed exactly how I needed to respond to my friend. I wasn't to rush in and "carry" her, but I was to be ready to help—if needed. That settled, I sang the next hymn with even greater enthusiasm.

To Ponder:

Do you ever wonder just how much help you should offer to someone who seems to go from crisis to crisis?

Have you ever tried to rescue someone, only to have the help backfire?

What balance between help and independence have you needed in your own life?

Impossible Standards

It is for freedom that Christ has us set us free.
Stand firm, then, and do not let yourselves
be burdened again by a yoke of slavery.
GALATIANS 5:1

At the end of a women's retreat at which I had told my usual Mama Farley stories, several women stayed behind to talk to me. One young woman kept letting the others go ahead, so I inwardly began to pray for her, wondering what terrible sin she wanted to confess without additional hearers. Finally she and I were alone.

As I turned to her, she blurted, "I'm not as close to the Lord as I used to be."

I often hear that statement, and it's usually followed by an admission of sin. So, bracing myself, I asked why she felt that way.

She began to twist the tissue in her hands. "I'm not spending enough time in the Word. I used to spend at least an hour studying the Bible every morning, but I don't now." Tears were beginning to form in her eyes.

That wasn't what I expected. "Tell me about your life," I invited.

"Well, I got married four years ago," she said, "and now we have three children—three, two, and one."

Astonished, I interrupted her. "Honey, you don't have *time* to spend an hour in the Word each morning."

Retreat speakers aren't supposed to say things like that, so I tried again: "Perhaps you could post Scriptures throughout the house to ponder as you go through your busy days."

She shook her head, so I scrambled for another idea. "What if you saw the care of your children as part of your daily worship of the Lord? As your little ones look to you in trust, that will be a reminder you are trusting your heavenly Father in the same way." I knew that was stretching the point, but she was desperate.

Tears were about to fall onto her cheeks. "But I want to be a godly woman like your grandmother," she said. "And there's no way she could have been that godly without spending *at least* an hour in the Word each day."

I smiled as I opened my arms to her. "Honey, I *know* she didn't spend an hour in the Word each day. Mama couldn't read."

At that, the young, tired mother threw herself against my shoulder, sobbing in relief and suddenly encouraged about her daily schedule. The truth about my godly grandmother had freed her from a standard that was quite impossible for her to achieve at her difficult stage of life. And I like to think that truth also made her a more relaxed, fun-loving mother.

To Ponder:

*Have you ever tried maintaining an impossible standard?
If so, what was behind your unrealistic expectations?
What helps you keep a balanced routine today? What
improvements are you still trying to make?
How would you have answered this young mother's
concerns?*

Kindness Spoken Here

*Better a dry crust with peace and quiet than
a house full of feasting, with strife.*
PROVERBS 17:1

In the entryway of Martha's home is a flowered wall hanging that reads *Kindness Spoken Here.* Many of the stitches are crooked and oversized, but the words are still prominently displayed.

Martha explained: "A couple of years ago, I was under a lot of stress in my job. That spilled into my relationship with my husband and my children and then in turn adversely affected their relationships with each other. Soon our home boiled with squabbles caused by the tension."

She frowned, remembering. "Finally my husband and I had a long talk. The result was that I got out my needlework basket and came up with this. Then every time someone was unkind to another—and I included myself in that rule—he or she had to retreat to a quiet room to pray and embroider one letter or part of a flower."

Martha smiled as she pointed to the design. "By the time all of us had worked on this for a while, the stitches got smaller, and so did our stress, as we finally understood what we were allowing it to do to us."

Stress is a reality in today's world—job stress, school stress, schedule stress, emotional stress—and, unfortunately, it finds its way into many homes. By itself, stress won't destroy our families; but the way we handle it can. Maybe it's time for all of us to work on a *Kindness Spoken Here* pattern.

To Ponder:

Has a job situation ever created tension in your home?
What steps do you take to eliminate tension in your home?
What do you wish you'd known earlier about how tension affects relationships?

The Subway Singer

The cheerful heart has a continual feast.
PROVERBS 15:15

One year, when my teens and I lived an hour north of New York City, we ventured down to Broadway to watch the Macy's Thanksgiving Day Parade with friends—and countless others. It was a memorable day of seeing floats and giant balloons that had long been part of our holiday, but only through TV. The best part of the trip, though, was the lesson I learned from a subway elevator operator.

For long hours each day, he was trapped in that box under the city streets, breathing air thick with fumes and dirt. I wouldn't have blamed him if he'd been grumpy as we boarded his elevator. But he greeted us cheerfully and asked where we were from.

When he had delivered us to our requested level, he wished us well, asked us to come again, and added a cheerful "I luv ya."

Later as we were waiting for the subway train on the lower level, we could hear him singing as he strolled in front of the elevator, waiting for his next load of passengers. Rather than allow himself to be bitter about his lot in life, he chose to bring freshness and joy to those who shared his day, even for those few moments.

What a challenge for me! What if, instead of fretting about my struggles, I chose to become like that subway singer and give others reason to smile at my memory?

To Ponder:

Have you ever had your day brightened by someone who was just enjoying his job?

How do you make a difficult task more bearable?

What do you think others see as they watch you at work?

Do You Have a "Yes" Face?

*You will receive a rich welcome into the eternal kingdom
of our Lord and Savior Jesus Christ.*
2 PETER 1:11

Now that I'm a "veteran" mom and my children are wonderfully grown and married, I'm often asked to speak to parenting groups about ways to keep the lines of communication open between the generations. At these gatherings, I enjoy sharing a story our former pastor told in one of his sermons:

Rain had fallen for several days as President Thomas Jefferson and his party traveled cross-country on horseback. Finally, they reached the river they were to cross and found the rain-swollen waters had swept away their only bridge.

The president and his entourage wandered up and down the riverbank awhile until they discovered a place where their horses could safely take them across. Nearby, a man sat hunched under a tree. He stood up as he saw the group approach and looked into the face of each man.

Then he spoke to President Jefferson. "Please, sir, will you carry me across the river with you?"

President Jefferson nodded and helped the man swing up behind him. When they arrived safely on the far bank, the man jumped down and offered his thanks.

One of Jefferson's escorts turned to the now-dismounted rider and challenged him: "How is it you dared to ask to ride behind the president of the United States?"

The man blanched, looked into the kind face of his benefactor, then faced his questioner.

"I didn't know I was speaking to the president," he said. "It's just that as I looked at each of you, I saw *no* in your faces and I saw *yes* in his."

As parents and friends, we display that all-important *yes* when we listen with our eyes as well as our ears—when our eight-year-old son gives a report of his day; when we push aside the stack of bills at month's end and gesture toward the chair when our sixteen-year-old daughter comes into the kitchen; when we ask our neighbor's opinion about the theme we were thinking of for the women's retreat. The people around us need more than just to *hear* of our love and concern for them. They need to *see* it in our faces.

To Ponder:

Have you, like the man in this account, asked for help based on the body language of another?

How do you typically respond when asked for help? How would you like to respond?

Has a stranger ever asked for your help? What was the situation?

What Voices Do You Listen To?

And this is my prayer: that your love may abound
more and more in knowledge and depth of insight,
so that you may be able to discern what is best
and may be pure and blameless until the day of Christ.
PHILIPPIANS 1:9-10

Lately, whenever I run into anyone predicting failure for my latest venture, I try to remember the story my friend Kim Crabill told about her son, Trey, who was pitching in the Little League championship game. The tying run was on third base, the winning run on second. On the mound, the pitcher leaned toward home plate, trying to concentrate on the catcher's signals for this last pitch of the game. All of a sudden the rooters for the opposing team began to boo, jeering, "Loser! You'll never get it over the plate!"

Trey narrowed his eyes and made an effort to block out the catcalls. Just that morning, on their way to the park, his mother had sensed his anxiety and asked him what was wrong.

"I hate it when the other team's fans yell at me," he confided.

"Do they come onto the field and yell in your face?" she asked, feigning naïveté.

"No."

"Can they take away your ability?"

"Well, no," he conceded. "But they make me feel bad, and I can't concentrate."

"Don't listen to their voices," his mom said. "Look at your catcher. Think about that next pitch. Their voices can't take away your ability; they can't stop you. But they *can* cause you to stop yourself."

Now, on the mound, Trey stared at the batter, went into his windup—and delivered strike three to win the game.

Like that young pitcher, most of us face tough challenges from time to time. And often we, too, can hear the jeers from a crowd that may not want us to win. Sometimes the voices come down to us from the distant past—the drunken parent, the cruel classmate, the unstable coworker. Those voices are hard to block out, and they can thwart our most determined efforts—if we let them.

If you're facing a challenge, pray, read the Word, seek godly counsel. But also make sure you're listening to the right voices—and not the ones that can make you stop yourself.

To Ponder:

When are you most vulnerable to negative voices from the past?

How do you deal with the "loser" feelings negative voices might stir up?

What, if any, Scriptures have you found helpful in countering those voices?

A Second Chance

Each of us should please his neighbor for his good,
to build him up.
ROMANS 15:2

I like the story I heard years ago about Thomas Edison. The famous inventor had spent thousands of hours experimenting with incandescent light. Now it appeared he had at last hit upon the solution he sought. With his staff clustered around him, Mr. Edison picked up the crystal bulb and passed it to his assistant, who was to attach it to a stand. Then the excited, nervous assistant dropped it!

Of course, everyone gasped as they saw the crystal shatter, but Mr. Edison merely patted the trembling young man on the shoulder and directed the fashioning of another bulb. When that one was ready, the staff gathered a second time, with the nervous assistant standing on the outside of the circle. But Mr. Edison called him forward and handed *him* the second bulb!

What a statement that made to the young assistant. And what a statement to his coworkers! Would I have handed the second bulb to the assistant? Would you? Of course, we say that people are more important than things, but what comes out of our mouth when our child drops the serving dish? Or when our guest breaks the ceramic figure we've had since childhood? And even if we do manage to say the right thing, do we hand the item to the erring individual the second time? Or do we say, "That's all right, dear. I'll do it"?

One of my goals in life is to get to the place where I can hand the "second bulb" to the one who dropped it the first time.

How about you?

To Ponder:

Have you ever "dropped the bulb"? What was the situation?

Did someone give you a second chance? How would you have liked the situation to have been handled?

Have you ever had an opportunity to encourage someone who has failed?

THE GIFT OF
FAMILY

Mysterious Flutterings

When Elizabeth heard Mary's greeting, the baby leaped in her
womb, and Elizabeth was filled with the Holy Spirit.
LUKE 1:41

My area of town seems to have taken seriously the Genesis directive to "be fruitful and multiply," and I often encounter glowing mothers-to-be at the mall or in the post office line. Even though it's been almost three decades since I was pregnant, I always smile at the young women as I recall those long-ago moments of wonder—moments spent pondering the mysterious multiplication of cells producing my baby.

For the elderly Elizabeth, six months pregnant with a child she had given up hoping for, one of those mysterious moments came when she heard her cousin Mary's voice and then felt the movement of her unborn son, who would later be known as John the Baptist. This account is told only in the Gospel of Luke. Perhaps Luke, a doctor, was intrigued by the physical aspects of this phenomenon. He reports the child moved with such vigor that Elizabeth, under the guidance of the Holy Spirit, could offer the joyous affirmation her young cousin needed.

We don't know if this was the first time Elizabeth had felt the baby move, but we do know it was significant enough that it became a special moment. Ask most mothers when they first felt their unborn baby's movement and their countenance softens as they describe where they were. Even these many years later, I remember I was sitting at my classroom desk, greeting students as they came into junior English. I was wearing a pale green dress and had a 1970s lacy shawl over my shoulders. I held my breath as I felt the incredible tiny fluttering that seemed like butterfly wings beating deep within. The moment brought the most incredible knowledge: another being, a real person, was growing within the secret depths of my body. In that moment the same awe and joy that washed over Elizabeth—and surely every other mother throughout the ages—welled up in me.

To Ponder:

What joyful moment do you remember even years later?
Do you recall a time when new life—either physical or emotional—first stirred within you?
Which voices in your life do you associate with new life?

Created for God's Purpose

Then the word of the Lord came to me, saying, "Before
I formed you in the womb I knew you."
JEREMIAH 1:4-5

Before my late husband, Don, and I were married, he often
did substitute teaching in his hometown eighty miles away
from where I lived. One lunch hour he wrote to me: "I look
at these seventh-grade girls and wonder what our own little
Holly will be like." Then he related his dreams for the daughter we hoped to have someday. He described how he hoped
her personality—and the personalities of her future siblings—
would develop, the activities he wanted our children to
participate in, and the places he hoped we all would explore
together.

It would be nine more years before we could use the name
for our daughter. During that time of waiting, we had only
dreams to attach to a yet-unseen person, but we already knew
and loved her. As I read Jeremiah 1:4-5 during this time, I
was excited by God's declaration that not only had he known
the prophet Jeremiah before he was born, but he had, in fact,
been the one who formed him. This was no random act of
nature. Equally significant, Jeremiah, even as the unborn
child, was separated for God's righteous purpose.

Jeremiah, born about six hundred years before Jesus, was a prophet who repeatedly warned his people to turn from their sins and toward the one true God. Called the "weeping prophet," he didn't have an easy life, but his words, even so many centuries later, still offer direction in the midst of life's challenges. They hold out hope that our dreams will be birthed in God's time and in his beauty—just as our little Holly was.

To Ponder:

Have you ever had a long-held dream that was finally birthed? If so, what was it?

Have you ever experienced a moment in which you knew God had a calling upon your life?

Have you, like Jeremiah, ever wanted God to move a little faster? What was the situation?

Tender Regard

He said to his mother, "Dear woman, here is your son,"
and to the disciple, "Here is your mother."
JOHN 19:26-27

My headache was worse, so I was sprawled on the sofa, trying to rest while eighteen-month-old Jay played nearby. Even with my eyes closed, I knew he was playing with his blocks. Then I heard him meander over to his toy shelf. Moments later I felt his little hand on my forehead. When I opened my eyes, Jay tucked his favorite stuffed animal, a blue teddy bear appropriately named "Blue Bear," under my arm.

"All better?" he asked.

And suddenly I was.

As I think of that scene I wonder if Mary had headaches, too, when Jesus was a toddler. Did he bring his favorite toy to her? I like to think that even then his little hand on her forehead released her from the pain. Later, at the weddings of their friends, did he make sure she was seated comfortably at the women's table before he joined the men?

John's Gospel narrative of Jesus' crucifixion paints a powerful picture of a son—God's Son—concerned for his mother even as he faces death. Seeing Mary standing with

John the disciple, Jesus uses the traditional expression of respect as he calls her "woman" and presents her to John, the one who will now care for her as if he were her own son. To the very last, our Lord's earthly life demonstrated the priority he placed on relationships and his tender regard for others—an example that remains for us today, sometimes embodied in the small hands of a child.

To Ponder:

Has a child ever ministered to your needs? What was the situation?

What do you think Jesus was like as a child?

What example did Jesus set for all adult children in his regard for his mother?

What Babies Need Most

*Then Jesus said to his disciples: "Therefore I tell you,
do not worry about your life, what you will eat; or about your
body, what you will wear. Life is more than food,
and the body more than clothes."*

LUKE 12:22-23

Have you ever been determined to do something perfectly? Lisa made that resolution when she was pregnant with her first child. She spent hours in the baby section of the department store, making lists of everything she was convinced the child would need upon arrival home from the hospital. She was especially determined to buy the best maple crib and matching dresser, noting for future reference that the accompanying youth bed was available. After all, she wanted her child to have the very best. She wasn't going to settle for anything like her own childhood bed, a small mattress pushed into the corner of a tiled room.

Lisa had forgotten that her childhood was unhappy, not because of the lack of nice things, but rather because of the atmosphere of tension and her own feelings of neglect. Babies need love and security—not the biggest and the best in furniture and clothes.

In Luke 12:22-23 Jesus said we shouldn't concentrate on acquiring the unimportant things in life. I sometimes wonder what our families would be like if we replaced the accumulation of *things* with joy in each other and the trust that God has promised to provide everything we need. When we put our confidence in the wrong things, we push the Lord's work to a secondary place, and we miss his unfailing peace.

Our little ones won't be with us forever. When they're grown, they won't remember whether they had size one designer jeans or a solid-maple crib. But they will remember, even subconsciously, whether they were loved and protected.

To Ponder:

Have you ever made a purchase trying to compensate for a childhood lack?

What guidelines do you try to use for purchases you make?

Do your childhood disappointments affect your approach to parenting your own children?

If I Had It to Do Over

They can train the younger women
to love their husbands and children.
TITUS 2:4

If I could redo any period in my life, I'd choose those
exhausting years when Jay and Holly were toddlers. I wish
I'd worried less about the house and what people thought
of me and concentrated more on enjoying my two little
people. As I look back, I don't remember which church
committees I served on or even who attended the deacon-
board gatherings I hosted in our dining room when my
husband was the chairman.

But I do remember special moments with our toddlers.
During one morning walk, the three of us gathered an armful
of Queen Anne's lace from a vacant lot and hurried home to
stick the blossoms in four vases of colored water—red, blue,
green, and yellow. Then both children leaned on the table,
their round faces resting on their hands as they watched the
lacy petals absorb the color of the water. I wish we'd picked
an even bigger bouquet that day. Those toddlers grew up
rather quickly, entered school, went away to college, married.
The only thing left of that day is the memory.

I can't call those years back, but they can be redeemed if

43

any tired young mother learns from my mistakes and enjoys the short years she has with her children. That's the message Paul offers in Titus 2:4 as he suggests that the mature spiritual women instruct the younger wives in the responsibilities and privileges of Christian womanhood. The older woman's years of Bible study and practical experience allow her to pass on valuable wisdom to those just starting out. If the younger women don't learn from the older ones, they run the risk of concentrating on the wrong priorities. But what a privilege God has given me, as a Titus 2:4 woman, to encourage the younger women around me to make wise choices—which may even include picking a weedy bouquet every now and then.

To Ponder:

What periods in your life do you sometimes wish you could redo?

Have you ever struggled with a hectic schedule? How did you deal with it?

What advice do you have for busy young parents?

A Precious Gift

Here am I, and the children God has given me.
HEBREWS 2:13

The couple kept pacing near gate 7 as we awaited the plane from Seattle. Occasionally the young woman would look at her husband for reassurance. He'd put his arm around her, kiss her forehead, and the pacing would begin again. At last the plane touched down and began taxiing to the gate. The young couple embraced as they watched the door. The young woman was trembling.

The gate representative approached, saying, "She'll be the last one off. An attendant will bring her."

Then she hugged the woman and added, "Don't worry. You guys will be great parents."

Parents! They were waiting to receive the child they were going to adopt. By now everyone's attention was directed to the door. We watched every passenger get off. Then finally a flight attendant came up the jet way carrying a dark-haired little girl about a year old. Gently, she handed the blinking child to her delighted parents.

What could be more precious than the life of a little one— whether that child is born to us, comes to us through adoption, or joins the family of believers through our witness? In Hebrews 2:13 and the surrounding verses, we are reminded of Christ's life on earth as he took human form to identify with our struggles and willingly became the sacrifice for our sins. The words from this verse are also found in Isaiah 8:18, where the thought is presented that we are members of a common family, acknowledging a common Father.

I can't imagine anything more profound than presenting our children—both our own sons and daughters and those whose lives we are privileged to touch—to our heavenly Father, not only here on earth but in heaven. How wonderful to be able to say when we stand before almighty God, "Here am I and the children whom you gave to me."

To Ponder:

Have you awaited the biological, adoptive, or spiritual arrival of a child? If so, what was the situation?
What is the toughest part of such waiting?
What do you want to be able to say when you stand before the Lord?

Careful—You're Being Watched!

Train a child in the way he should go,
and when he is old he will not turn from it.
PROVERBS 22:6

One evening several years ago, I was especially troubled about a looming decision, so I retreated to my bedroom to read the Word and jot down verses that spoke to my dilemma. I picked up the old white Bible on my nightstand. A couple of other Bibles were there, newer translations, but this was the Bible I'd had since the seventh grade. Its verses were underlined, its margins written in, its cover worn. Further, this was the Bible I had carried on my wedding day. A florist had covered it with clear plastic and pinned the orchids on it. Now I picked it up, searching through its worn pages for an answer to this latest challenge.

Within a few minutes, my then ten-year-old son, Jay, came up the stairs looking for me. His nine-year-old sister, Holly, intercepted him in the hallway.

"Don't bother Mom," she said. "She's reading the Bible—her *white* one."

I heard Jay exclaim, "Oh!" and go back downstairs. I hadn't realized anyone noticed which Bible I read when I was the most troubled. But our children, even at a young age, observe far more than we think they do. In a way, it's an unsettling thought: Our actions impact our kids more than the most eloquent lecture ever could. Like it or not, they will follow our example—for better and for worse.

So maybe the next time we're tempted to complain about that irritating person at church, or turn on that questionable TV sitcom, or snap at our spouse, we'll remember that there are little eyes watching us and little minds taking it all in. Yes, it's a responsibility—but it's also a God-given privilege.

To Ponder:

Have you noticed one of your kids picking up a bad habit of yours? How did you handle it?

Who in your childhood modeled positive and negative behaviors?

What do you do when you find yourself doing the same things that bothered you in your own parents?

Child Labor Is Okay

Now we ask you . . . to respect those who work hard among you, who are over you in the Lord and who admonish you.
1 THESSALONIANS 5:12

Why is it that we parents often think we have to do everything ourselves? Actually, experts tell us that youngsters with time on their hands aren't happy, and those with no responsibilities tend to quarrel much more than those who are busy around the house.

But while we're setting up guidelines for chores, we need to make sure the kids understand exactly what we expect from them. In other words, we usually can't just say, "Clean your room."

We need to give specifics: "Make up your bed. Hang up your clean clothes. Put the dirty ones in the hamper. Put away the toys. Dust the dresser, chair, and shelves."

When my children were young, they liked having a list on the kitchen counter so they could cross off each item as they finished. I found that worked better than just giving them another chore after they'd finished the first one. If they kept getting a string of jobs, they'd feel defeated, thinking work would never end. All of us, even children, need to see we have a reachable goal.

I also found they worked best if I worked with them. So when they were first learning to work, I couldn't just announce, "Put all your toys on the shelf." I needed to say, *"Let's* put your toys away." Sometimes I'd even set the timer, and we'd make a game out of putting everything away within a specified number of minutes.

And even young children can be in charge of an occasional meal that doesn't require cooking. There's nothing wrong with cold chicken sandwiches—or even peanut butter—for dinner, either. The first meals my youngsters put together were rather interesting: sixth-grader Holly enjoyed trying simple cookbook recipes and trading ideas with her friends. But on Jay's night to prepare dinner, he would serve whatever was in the refrigerator. He gradually progressed, though, from warmed-over pizza to spicy potatoes and a marvelous cheese-broccoli soup.

Don't hesitate to include children in the day-to-day responsibilities. Together, everyone wins.

To Ponder:

What techniques have you found useful as you teach children to work?

What do you find the most frustrating as you teach a new skill to someone else?

What changes would you like to make in your interaction with those you are trying to teach?

Out of the Mouths of Babes

Pride goes before destruction, a haughty spirit before a fall.
PROVERBS 16:18

Are you ever tempted to pull your kids into your schemes?
Believe me, you don't even want to try. Years ago, our family
attended the annual Memorial Day dinner at a Michigan
Bible conference. Knowing I would be surrounded by good
Dutch cooks, I worried about what to take. I pored over my
cookbooks before deciding on a hot chicken casserole. I baked
it carefully, sprinkled the cheese on top just so, then showed
the dish to my husband, saying, "This is ours—make sure you
take a lot of it when you go through the line."

When we arrived at the dinner, Don and Jay went on
ahead, while Holly and I lingered to chat with friends. When
we finally went through the line and arrived at my chicken
dish, sure enough, there were only two scoops taken out. My
worst potluck fear was about to come true: I was going to
have to take home an almost-full pan.

Trying to hide my chagrin, I picked up the serving spoon and
said cheerfully to Holly, "This looks good, doesn't it, honey?"

Holly nodded, then chirped in her loud four-year-old voice,
"That's ours, huh, Mama?"

While my face turned red, the others nearby turned to smile at me. I had been caught.

See? If we try to involve children in our schemes, the plan will backfire every time.

To Ponder:

Have you ever tried to "pull a fast one" in front of a child?

Why do you think some of us are tempted to resort to such schemes?

What lessons in humility have you learned from children?

Aunt Sandra's Guide
to Successful Vacations

*The crooked roads shall become straight,
the rough ways smooth.*
LUKE 3:5

Planning a car trip? A l-o-n-g-g-g one? Ah, I remember those days all too well. But I also remember the effort I put into making those times not only bearable but even enjoyable.

We used to leave very early—even 3:30 in the morning—in order to take advantage of Jay's and Holly's sleeping time. We would tuck them into the seat belts with extra pillows around their heads, fold their "blankies" over their little legs, and go on our way.

We stopped often at rest stops to let both toddlers—and ourselves—run off pent-up energy. We always carried a red ball in the trunk so our little ones could chase it at each stop, and we quickly learned not to allow ourselves to be talked into letting the ball go into the backseat, since it inevitably ended up bouncing off the driver's head.

I used to have little wrapped games available for those late-morning times when little hands were starting to stray

53

toward the sibling's ribcage. And I'd use the gifts as incentives, too, for good behavior.

Stopping early at a motel each night ensured not only that we'd get a room but that we parents would get enough sleep to be able to get up early the next morning and start the adventure again.

Yes, the struggles—and joys—of family vacations *will* pass, so soak up each adventure now. I assure you, these times will someday be included in your fond memories.

To Ponder:

What do you dread most about family trips?
How do you prepare for these adventures?
What have you recently learned about traveling that you wish you had known years ago?

Pick Your Battles

Fathers, do not not exasperate your children; instead, bring
them up in the training and instruction of the Lord.
EPHESIANS 6:4

While I waited to board my flight, I watched a father and daughter near me. The girl was about ten, with long dark hair framing her face. I couldn't hear the father's words but saw him gesture to the child's pocket, then indicate he wanted her to pull back her hair. As the girl shook her head, the father took a threatening step toward her. With set jaw, she pulled the clip from her pocket and arranged her hair to his liking.

I was saddened by the scene. Granted, I didn't have the whole story, but it seemed as though too much attention was directed toward one unimportant item—the girl's hair. Her chosen style wasn't offensive to anyone but her father.

In my mind, this man had violated a basic, commonsense rule of parenting: *Pick your battles.* By going nose to nose over this issue, he had created a destructive atmosphere of criticism, intimidation, and fear. I have no doubt that in time, his attitude will not only provoke his child to wrath but may even color her attitudes toward the opposite sex in general.

What if that father instead had offered encouragement, patience, and love? Like it or not, a child's first understanding of God is influenced by his or her relationship with an earthly father. I wish the man in the airport had taught his daughter about acceptance—first his own and then, through loving example, God's. What a difference that would have made, not only in settling that day's unimportant battle, but in resolving those *important* battles still in the future.

To Ponder:

Have you ever witnessed a parent's power struggle with a child? Were you ever that parent?

What do you consider the most important values in child rearing?

If you're a veteran parent, what would you say to a new mom or dad about these issues?

Calling In the Experts

*Pride only breeds quarrels, but wisdom is found
in those who take advice.*
PROVERBS 13:10

When Jay was thirteen, I struggled with finding the balance between letting him have fun and forcing him to be, as he put it, "a wimp."

Our discussions in this area were futile. Then one afternoon while we were vacationing at Lake Michigan, Jay came in from the beach all excited about a new game he and his friends had—a game whose "fun" consisted of jumping out of a moving boat.

Horrified, I gave the typical, cautious-mother arguments about the danger of what he was doing. But he insisted he could "handle it."

At that point, I launched into an account of a brilliant former student who had died in a freak accident at his college. I even told about one of our distant relatives who had been killed by the motor on his own boat when he fell into the lake.

Still, Jay remained adamant that he and his friends would be fine. I was just worrying too much, he told me. Stymied, I breathed a quick prayer. Then in a sudden burst of inspiration, I called the coast guard, explained the situation, and asked if I was overreacting. The officer assured me I wasn't and added that not only were the boys' activities stupid, but they were a good way to get *killed*.

I asked if he'd tell Jay what he had just told me.

"You better believe it," he replied. "Put him on."

Jay was on the phone for several minutes, listening intently, and occasionally answering, "Yes. . . . Yes, *sir*," as the officer gave him details of accidents just off our shore. As far as I know, the boys didn't play the game again.

I like to think that call may very well have saved their lives. And I remember the idea to make it came only after I prayed for help.

To Ponder:

Do you think parents have a tendency to overreact when they learn of their teen's activities?

How would you have handled the situation of the boys jumping off a moving boat?

Have you ever called an expert to back you up? If so, was it helpful?

Prayers, Not Lectures

*I urge, then, first of all, that requests, prayers, intercession
and thanksgiving be made for everyone.*
1 TIMOTHY 2:1

Are you ever tempted to tell someone what to do? I certainly am. But occasionally I try to remember an important lesson my mother taught me years ago.

It was a cold, rainy Saturday morning when I finally looked at the cluttered bedroom I had shared with my husband. It had been more than a year since his death to brain cancer, but I was only now realizing how crowded the room was with my little bed next to the one he had slept in during his long illness. For those many months, I had found it less traumatic to just ignore the larger bed we had shared for more than sixteen years.

But that morning, with eleven-year-old Jay helping, I tackled the clutter with determination. Soon the phone rang. It was my mother.

"You sound out of breath, honey," she said. "Did you have to run up the stairs to answer?"

"No. Jay and I were just shoving furniture around," I said. "I'm rearranging my bedroom and taking down the little bed."

My mother started to cry. "Mother, please don't do that,"

I pleaded. "You know I can't stand it when you cry long-distance."

Finally she could talk. "It's just that I'm happy the Lord answered my prayer," she said. "When I was over there last week and helping you fold clothes, I looked at that crowded room and asked the Lord to help you rearrange the room and go back to your old bed. And every morning since then, that's been my prayer."

The news startled me, of course, but it also got me to thinking. What if she had marched in and said, "You've ignored this room long enough. It's time to get on with your life"? I'm convinced that approach wouldn't have worked since the "letting go" would have been from her insistence rather than my own readiness.

No, a wise woman chose to ask the Lord to move a hurting daughter forward—and he did. May we remember that when we're tempted to tell folks what their next step must be.

To Ponder:

Do you ever get impatient when someone isn't moving through grief as rapidly as you think he or she should?

Have your good intentions in telling someone what to do ever backfired?

What have you found to be the best solution when you want someone to move forward emotionally?

A Good Name

A good name is more desirable than great riches; to be esteemed is better than silver or gold.

PROVERBS 22:1

With each of my published books, I insist that my unusual maiden name—Picklesimer—be included on the title page as part of my byline. Occasionally, someone will mistakenly accuse me of being a "flaming feminist" because I ask for its inclusion. Usually, I ignore such thoughtless comments, but occasionally—if I'm in the right mood—I'll tell the whole story:

The day I came home from having met Doris Schumacher, the woman who gave me the vision to get an education, I told my parents I was going to be a teacher "just like Doris." Making such an announcement took gumption because until the late 1950s, none of the women in my family had attended college. In fact, several hadn't even graduated from high school, since many of the relatives felt that education was wasted on those who "just" got married and took care of a family. After all, they said, a college degree wouldn't help you grow a better garden or raise prettier babies. So after I declared my intentions, I held my breath, wondering how my dad would react.

"Well, good for you," he said. "Get all the education you can. I wish I'd been able to get more." Then he continued. "But you need to know I won't be able to help you. In fact, when I die, the only thing I will be able to leave you is my name. Take care of it."

In the many years since that scene, my education has opened incredible doors that even my childhood fantasies couldn't include. And I'm grateful to say I've never brought dishonor to the name *Picklesimer*. Now I'm determined that if I can bring some small amount of *honor* to it by including it in the front of my books, I will do exactly that!

The greater implication, of course, is that if I am concerned about taking care of my *earthly* father's name, how much more I should be concerned about taking care of my *heavenly* Father's name.

Each new day provides yet more opportunities to bring disgrace or honor to his name. The choice rests with us.

To Ponder:

Have you ever received special instructions to take care of something important to a family member? What were the circumstances?

How would you like your family name to be remembered?

What are some ways you can protect your heavenly Father's name?

A Prayer Armistice

Be at peace with each other.
MARK 9:50

It had been another one of those frustrating days when I didn't need to face two warring teens. As soon as I came through the door, though, they both wanted to tell their side of the story—namely whose turn it was to get the TV.

Understanding mother that I am, I spouted something close to, "You guys must hold secret meetings at night to see how you can drive me nuts!"

I didn't even have my coat off yet, but we sat on the carpeted stairs as I listened to one side and then to the other. Then I mumbled, "I gotta pray about this."

Still on the stairs, I started with a simple "Father, you know I hate days like this. I identify more with Saul's craziness than Solomon's wisdom, so please show me how to solve this."

Jay and Holly didn't offer to pray then, and I didn't make them. They needed space and time to think. I sent them to their rooms, said no one was watching TV for the rest of the evening, and added that I didn't want to see them until dinner, thirty minutes later. We'd work out a schedule then.

Meanwhile, as I tossed salad and cooked pasta, I kept talking to the Lord. In the midst of my emotional hand-wringing came the solution: odd and even days. Jay was born on October 5, and Holly on February 18, so on odd days of the week, Jay could choose the TV shows and sit in the front seat as we drove to school, but he would also be expected to help prepare dinner. The same would happen for Holly on the even days. A simple solution, certainly, but one I'm convinced I never would have discovered without praying about my frustration.

A few weeks later, at a mothers' luncheon, I shared my honest prayer and the solution that came from it. Afterward, another mother, apparently missing the point that my solution came through prayer, scolded me for not making my children pray aloud when I was first confronted with their argument. She declared that she *always* made her children pray aloud when there was any disagreement, and as a result, her children never even raised their voices in the house. (She also let me know if I were a truly spiritual mother, my children would have done the right thing immediately.)

I asked how old her children were.

"Six and nine," she answered.

I patted her arm. "That's wonderful," I said. But what I meant was "Let's talk again in about seven years."

To Ponder:

Have you ever been confronted with an argument you were expected to settle? What was the situation?

What solutions have you found for seemingly impossible situations?

How do you respond to people who think their solutions are more "spiritual" than yours?

Know When to Lighten Up

*Pleasant words are a honeycomb, sweet to the soul
and healing to the bones.*
PROVERBS 16:24

I'm all for teaching children about consequences. But sometimes a little tolerance accomplishes a lot, too. . . .

One morning when my daughter was in the seventh grade,
I opened the refrigerator to get my lunch for work and
discovered she had forgotten hers. I stood in front of the open
refrigerator for a long time, arguing with myself. Should I
ignore the bag and let her go hungry to teach her a lesson?
On the other hand, this was only the first time this had
happened. Mercy won out: I decided that if this became a
habit, we'd deal with it then. Besides, I was going to suffer
more than she would if I left her lunch in the refrigerator.

I arrived at her school just a few minutes before her first
class began. She and several of her friends were still by their
lockers, chatting about the day's plans. Holly turned just as
I approached. She was delighted to see me and thanked me
profusely for bringing her lunch, saying she'd made egg salad
and had been disappointed to discover she'd left it at home.

I was happy I'd chosen grace over strictness, but another
parenting dilemma remained: how not to embarrass my

middle schooler in public. Our long-standing custom had been to hug good-bye, but after I handed her the lunch and heard one more thank you, *I stood there awkwardly for a moment. I wanted that hug, but . . .*

Finally I said, "Well, I'm off to work. Who wants a hug before I go?"

Kristi hopped up from the floor. "I do!" I gave her a motherly bear hug, while Holly stood by, red-faced at another of her mom's antics.

Then Jessica said, "Me, too." One by one, I gave her five friends a squeeze to send them into the day. Holly and I hugged last, and I hurried out the door.

That evening, as we cleared the table after dinner, she again thanked me for having taken her lunch to school. I said I hoped I hadn't embarrassed her with all of the hugs.

She shook her head. "Oh, you did at first because you're always doing weird things. But later, two of my friends said you're pretty neat. I just agreed with them."

I gave her another hug right then.

To Ponder:

How do you decide when to let your children accept the consequences of an action and when to exercise "grace"?

Is it ever okay to bend parenting rules? If so, when? If not, why?

Have you ever struggled between showing affection for your child and not wanting to embarrass him or her in front of friends? What happened?

No Lectures

For if you forgive men when they sin against you, your heavenly Father will also forgive you.
MATTHEW 6:14

It had been another of those frustrating times as a parent as I wondered about the fine line between the *teaching* of "How can we solve this?" and the *lecturing* of "I knew that would happen!" Then my friend Tom Youngblood told me a story from his youth that gave me a new perspective:

When Tom was seventeen, his father, Chester, bought a new truck. He had always driven secondhand pickups but suddenly, to everyone's amazement, had purchased a new green Ford. Not only was it shiny, new, and perfect, it even had a radio—quite a luxury for the man who had always driven vehicles Tom considered "rusty and wired together."

One evening Tom had been invited to have dinner with his girlfriend's family, so he borrowed the new truck. Chester knew his son would drive carefully, especially since the snows had been heavy that year—even by western Pennsylvania standards.

The first few miles were uneventful, but just a couple of miles from Tom's destination, a snowplow started down the hill toward him. Wanting to take no chances with blades that appeared menacingly oversized, Tom pulled to the side of the road.

After a long moment, the plow passed safely, and Tom gently pressed the accelerator. But the snow had hidden the shallow ditch he had pulled into. He gave the gas pedal a little extra pressure. Suddenly the truck spun out of the incline, fishtailed, then banged into the guardrail.

Tom's stomach churned as he got out to look at the back fender. Sure enough, the shiny green paint now had a serious dent and a long scratch. Tom let out a frustrated sigh, muttering, "Oh, brother."

Dinner with his girlfriend's family that evening was not fun. The roast beef seemingly had no taste. And Tom wasn't his usual jovial, talkative self. All he could think about was having to give an account of the accident. As he poked at the mashed potatoes on his plate, he thought of his robust iron-worker father's weekly routine that began with faithful attendance at the morning and evening church services. During the week, he worked long hours. On Saturdays, he was always doing things for others—helping them repair a roof or mend a fence. That was Tom's favorite day since he could work right next to the man who seemed to know how to do everything in the world. Finally, the silent dinner was over, and it was time for Tom to inch home. As he came in through the back door to the kitchen, his mother, Doris, took one look at his tormented expression and exclaimed, "What's wrong?"

Tom shook his head. "I banged up the back of the truck."

His mother gasped, "What happened?"

As Tom explained, his mother said, "Well, you've got to tell Dad. He's in the basement."

The walk from the kitchen to the basement seemed far too short. At the sound of Tom's footsteps on the stairs, Chester looked up from sharpening a saw. Immediately, Tom plunged into a rapid explanation of the snowplow and his failed attempt to protect the truck.

Chester's expression never changed. "Okay," he said and turned back to the saw. Tom stood there for a moment, stunned. His dad could be fast on the draw when it came to disciplining any of the three kids. This reaction was different.

Tom continued to wait awkwardly for a long moment, but Chester didn't comment further. Finally, Tom walked back up the stairs, marveling that his dad's understanding had far exceeded Tom's hopes. And he knew, based on his father's past actions, that he would not speak of this again. After all, what could he say that Tom hadn't already said to himself?

As Tom finished his story that day, he said, "I learned an important lesson in forgiveness—and my father never had to say a thing." Then he added, "Chances are, had he yelled or grounded me, the impact would not be as significant these decades later."

I leaned back in my chair, comparing his story to my parenting dilemma. So, good parenting doesn't say, "I told you so." Rather, it helps the child learn from—and build on— those inevitable mistakes. Suddenly, I had my answer. And I smiled.

To Ponder:

Have you ever had the dilemma of how much scolding or forgiveness you should offer?

Have you ever been surprised by someone's calm acceptance of your mistake? If so, what was the situation?

What did you learn from the situation that you now apply to your daily life?

The Apron Strings

But do not use your freedom to indulge
the sinful nature.
GALATIANS 5:13

When my son, Jay, graduated from high school, he, his sister, Holly, and I celebrated that evening at our favorite restaurant.

One present from me was a narrow box containing two strips of blue flowered material. As Jay folded back the tissue, he stared at the vaguely familiar pattern for a long moment. Finally I said, "That's my most important gift of all, honey. Those are my apron strings to symbolize that you're no longer tied to them."

Jay grinned, and Holly immediately exclaimed, "Great! Next year, do I get apron strings, too?" Groan. The years were passing far too quickly. But sure enough, just a few days later (it seemed), there we were again at our same favorite restaurant. This time it was Holly who was opening presents for *her* high school graduation. When she got to the narrow box, she smiled and quickly tore the paper off. Inside, indeed, were the strings from my second apron. Attached was this note:

Dear Holly,
As Jay can tell you, I'll often try to take this gift back.
But here are my apron strings to say that I am trying to
let you go. Go forward with God.
Much love, Mom

Both of those evenings were milestones in our finding new ways to relate—no longer just as parent and child, but as adult to adult. In the process of building new relationships with Jay and Holly over the years, I've discovered that these relationships are gifts to be treasured.

And, since those long-ago evenings, I've often thought about the celestial apron strings our heavenly Father has given us. He protects us, yes, but he also gives us freedom. Freedom to choose our daily routines, freedom to spend time with him (or not), even freedom to discard his loving guidelines. At times, I wish he had never cut those strings for me, since I haven't always chosen the right way. But his empowering us with choice should be encouraging, too: it says we *can* choose the right way, including choosing to have a fuller relationship with him. And that's a great gift, indeed.

To Ponder:

What physical or spiritual milestones has your family faced?

Have you given or received symbolic gifts? If so, what were they?

What advice do you have for parents who struggle with letting go of their children?

A Faith of Your Own

I have been reminded of your sincere faith, which first lived
in your grandmother Lois and in your mother Eunice and,
I am persuaded, now lives in you also.

2 TIMOTHY 1:5

Even though I grew up in Michigan, we always vacationed
in Kentucky with my grandparents, Papa and Mama Farley.
In that mountain community, all I had to say was that I
was the granddaughter of Carter and Nancy Farley and the
daughter of their youngest child, Wilma. The questioner
would smile and launch into an account of my grandparents'
godly testimonies, my mother's gentle spirit, and my dad's
helpfulness. Because of the excellent reputation of these
important folks in my life, I was immediately accepted—and
watched out for.

I remember the first morning Mama allowed me to get the
mail from Box 4 in Miz Bailey's general store and post office.
All along the route, neighbors called out their greetings and
added warnings of the latest copperhead sightings near the
stone bridge. The one we called Granny Smith called me to
her gate and thrust a hearty piece of her renowned gingerbread into my hand. Another friend, Polly, waved from her
favorite spot on the porch and then launched into comments
about my latest growth spurt. Eventually, I made it to the

welcoming planks of Miz Bailey's porch, where she greeted me as warmly as she did any grownup.

Whenever I read of Paul's mentoring of Timothy, I think of the long-ago community that welcomed me. And just as Paul was confident the lad would be an asset to his ministry because of his family background, so I was accepted because of my family's good reputation—and then given an opportunity to prove my own worth.

I especially appreciate Paul's acknowledgment of the faith that *lived* in those important people in Timothy's life—not as an occasional visitor, but as an abiding presence. Although I know salvation can't be inherited from even the most godly relatives, I know their faith does affect the children who come after them. And I'm grateful, because my life is proof of a faithful heritage.

Perhaps the most important lesson to take away from this Scripture is this: While we can cherish the godly heritage or sterling reputation of those who have gone before, we need to live it out in our own lives. Yes, I'm proud of being recognized as the daughter and granddaughter of such well-regarded people as my parents and grandparents. I'm grateful for their examples. But the best way I can show my appreciation is to walk with my Lord day in, day out—continuing on the path they laid down for me.

To Ponder:

Is there anyone in your early life who set a godly example for you? How did he or she influence your growth in the Lord?

What influence have you had on another's life?

What would you like someone to say about your impact on him or her?

Three at the Altar

*A father to the fatherless, a defender of widows,
is God in his holy dwelling.*

PSALM 68:5

For sixteen years after Don's death, Jay, Holly, and I had
been a family of three, together facing cross-country moves,
financial crises, and life's various challenges. With the Lord's
help, we had climbed on top of our grief—or so I thought.
Then Holly got engaged.

As she and I were making wedding plans, I realized that
she seemed melancholy. Then, one evening, she lamented the
fact that her dad wasn't there to walk her down the aisle. We
both cried a little, but she wiped her eyes and determined to
ask Jay to escort her. I started praying right then that his
normal public reticence wouldn't keep him from acceding to
her wishes.

The next evening, the three of us gathered in the living
room, and Holly made her request. In anticipation of this, Jay
had prepared a little speech, but got only as far as "Holly,
that's Dad's job . . ." before she—in typical Aldrich family
style—stopped him from finishing his sentence.

"But Dad's dead!" she wailed.

"Believe me, Holly, I know," he sighed. "What I was going to say is that's Dad's role, but *Mom* has been the one who's held this family together. *She* should walk you down the aisle."

Now it was my turn to wail. "But Jay, I want to be the mother of the bride," I protested, ignoring the enormous compliment he had just given me. "I want to stand up and turn to watch Holly come down the aisle."

Poor Jay. He'd grown up with a mother, a sister, and a neutered cat—and now he had two crying women to calm down. While he patted first one, then the other on the shoulder, Holly and I blew our noses. Then we all settled down to discuss possible solutions. After my usual prayer of "Lord, please help," we finally decided we would "tag team" the event: Jay would walk Holly down the aisle to my pew; then I would step out and give the declaration in answer to the pastor's question "Who escorts this woman to this man?" (Notice we don't give away women in *this* family.)

No, the solution wasn't our first choice—that one had included Don—but it was a good one. In fact, as it turned out, the three of us standing together before the altar provided a touching visible symbol of the team we had been. And all because we invited the Lord into the problem, analyzed our choices, and adjusted to the solution. Not a bad combination in any situation.

To Ponder:

If you have lost a special person in your family, what times are toughest for you?

How have you adjusted?

What advice do you have for others facing a significant event after a loss?

THE JOY OF
THE LORD

Mama's Biscuits

*Let us be thankful, and so worship God acceptably
with reverence and awe.*
HEBREWS 12:28

Years ago I visited my Kentucky grandmother, Mama Farley, just after I had earned my master's degree. Even though she was in her early eighties then, Mama's zest for life and love for the Lord were matched only by her biscuit making.

The first morning I was awakened before six by sounds from the kitchen and hurriedly dressed, convinced I had overslept. Tugging at my sleeves, I stood in the kitchen archway a moment to catch my breath.

I noticed that Mama's back was a little more stooped and her hair whiter. Everything else was the same—even the wood-burning stove. As I watched, Mama pulled a skillet of beautiful biscuits from her trusty old oven. I would have placed them on the serving plate with a self-satisfied sigh. But Mama set them in the center of the table and whispered, "Thank you, Lord."

Her gentle words hit me like a rebuke. I backed into the hallway, tears filling my eyes. My life was heaped with material goods, and I had achieved an education Mama never could have dreamed of. But it had not occurred to me to thank God for his gifts.

Right there in the hallway, I quietly voiced my gratitude to him for my numerous blessings before hurrying into the kitchen to give my grandmother a hug. Today, whether paying bills, planting spring flowers, or pulling a pan of golden biscuits from my own oven, I think of Mama as I murmur my own "Thank you, Lord."

To Ponder:

Have you ever learned an important lesson from someone who wasn't aware of your presence? What was the scene?

What sometimes hinders you from giving thanks?

How could we teach our children a spirit of gratitude?

Isn't Jesus Sweet?

How beautiful on the mountains are the feet of those who
bring good news, who proclaim peace, who bring good tidings,
who proclaim salvation, who say to Zion, "Your God reigns!"
ISAIAH 52:7

In our little Kentucky community, the center of social and
religious life was Four Mile Missionary Baptist Church.
Perched on the bank of the Cumberland River, the little white
clapboard building had survived numerous floods, the Great
Depression, and even, in the 1950s, the repaving of the road
just outside its front door.

On Sunday mornings, the preacher would ring the bell
shortly after 9:30 to let folks know he had arrived. Soon the
community would gather, and we would greet those we
hadn't seen at Miz Bailey's store throughout the week. Sarah
would ask about ailing relatives or laugh appreciatively at the
latest grandbaby story. Minnie often pulled a promised quilt
pattern out of her pocket. Zelfie, my great-grandfather's sixth
wife, would nod shyly and go inside. Gradually we would all
meander into the church, where the fourteen square-back
pews made by my grandfather were arranged, seven on each
side. The men sat on the right, the women on the left.

If the dirt road leading from Mabel's house "up the holler"
wasn't muddy, she would arrive to play the out-of-tune

upright piano. If she couldn't come, Fred, the tall, dark-haired bass singer who always sat in the back, would lead us in "lining" the songs. Even now I can hear him leading us, phrase by phrase, in the singing of "A Beautiful Life":

> *Each day I'll do (each day I'll do)*
> *A golden deed (a golden deed),*
> *By helping those (by helping those)*
> *Who are in need (who are in need);*
> *My life on earth (my life on earth)*
> *Is but a span (is but a span),*
> *And so I'll do (and so I'll do)*
> *The best I can (the best I can).*

Then we'd all intone the chorus:

> *Life's evening sun (life's evening sun)*
> *Is sinking low (is sinking low),*
> *A few more days (a few more days)*
> *And I must go (and I must go)*
> *To meet the deeds (to meet the deeds)*
> *That I have done (that I have done),*
> *Where there will be (where there will be)*
> *No setting sun (no setting sun).*

Most of those I used to sing with as a child have gone on to where there is no setting sun. And the folks who were still there when the new road came through in '64 were forced to move. But all of them are still alive in my memory. In fact, whenever I'm tempted to complain "It's not fair" about some difficulty, I think of Elizabeth Smith. She was a sweet-faced lady in her late thirties who always wore her hair pulled back into the braided bun that was popular with our women. Even at the age of ten, I was taller than she was. You see, she was bent almost double and supported her body weight with a sturdy walking stick that was only about fifteen inches high. Leaning on her cane, she would look up at us with a smile, comment on the beauty of the day or the needed rain, and then offer a heartfelt "Isn't Jesus sweet?"

My aunt told me Elizabeth had been dropped by the "granny woman" who had attended her birth, and her little back had been broken. But while Elizabeth had every legitimate reason to complain about the tragedy that had altered her life forever, I never heard her grumble. Instead, she focused on the sweetness of the One whose presence was very real to her.

What would happen if those of us with far less to complain about took our cue from Elizabeth Smith? "Isn't Jesus sweet?" would certainly make a difference in any attitude.

To Ponder:

Do you have a favorite childhood memory of church?

Do you know someone who has every reason to complain, but doesn't? What has that person taught you?

What would you like the children you know in your church to remember about you?

The View above the Fog

Even the darkness will not be dark to you.
PSALM 139:12

In the midst of our battle with my husband's brain cancer, I was overwhelmed by worry and work. I was emotionally and physically drained. One morning I left for school in a dense late-autumn fog. Everything was so murky I had to drive by instinct on the back road. After proceeding at a creep for several minutes, I guessed the stop sign should be just ahead. Ah, there it was.

As I edged the car forward, I decided the fog wouldn't be as heavy on top of the overpass. At least I'd be able to see from there. I inched to the top—and was treated to an incredible sight. The little valleys surrounding the expressway brimmed with pink mist rather than gray gloom. Above the mysterious mist the sun's rays streamed through gorgeous purple and orange clouds. I gasped at the spectacle.

Down below, cars crawled through the murk I had just escaped. *If only they could have this view!*

When I had to leave the overpass and descend into the fog again, the memory of the beautiful scene went with me. I continued to school, strangely refreshed. I knew that even as our family struggled through our own darkness, God would grant us glimpses of light. I just hadn't made it to a place where I could see above the fog.

Since that gloomy day, I've learned to do several things when I struggle to find my way out of a personal fog:

- *Pray—a lot!* The Lord helps us, but we have to ask him for help.
- *Draw strength and inspiration from Scripture.* Many folks in the Bible also faced tough situations, but God brought them through.
- *Don't expect others to meet every need.* Even the most loving family member or friend can't be all we need. Only the Father never sleeps and is available to strengthen and guide us twenty-four hours a day.
- *Help others.* As I reach out to encourage others who might be facing trials, I find myself encouraged, too.
- *Choose the right attitude.* I do have choices in life, even if it's nothing more than how I choose to react to my circumstances. Life is often difficult and stressful, but I can choose to trust in the good that the Lord can bring from it.

To Ponder:

Have you ever been surprised by a beautiful scene? If so, describe it.

Has a scene in nature ever offered peace or hope as you faced a tough situation? What emotional help did you gain from that scene?

What do you do when you can't see your way out of a struggle?

In God's Image

Then God said, "Let us make man in our image,
in our likeness."
GENESIS 1:26

Our son, Jay, was born one bright October morning. As I
heard him yell in protest at being thrust from his warm, dark
sanctuary into the cold, yellow delivery room, the doctor said,
"You have a son. And he's perfect."

But *hearing* of his perfection couldn't compare to that
moment when the nurse handed him to me.

I looked at this brand-new being and whispered, "Hello,
sweetheart," and kissed his tiny hands.

In the years since Jay's and Holly's births, I've often
pondered the incredible idea that we humans are created in
God's image. As he speaks in Genesis 1:26, I'm convinced he
was talking not only to the rest of the Trinity (Jesus and the
Holy Spirit) but to the angels—the entire host of heaven—as
well.

Only Jesus would later have an earthly body, so the
"image" spoken of here undoubtedly refers to the human's
ability to think, hear, see, and speak. But to be created in the
image of God also means we have the ability—and privilege—
of knowing, loving, and serving him. What a difference that

understanding should make in how we live our life and in how we react to others. After all, if we remember that every human life was created to be a reflection of our heavenly Father, our reactions to others have to be coated by his love. And such awareness can be as sweet as the moment when we first kiss a newborn's tiny fingers.

To Ponder:

In what circumstances are you best reminded of God's perfect creation?

What do you think "created in God's image" includes?

What characteristic of God's image do you most want in your own life?

Sorting the Wonders

But Mary treasured up all these things
and pondered them in her heart.
LUKE 2:19

Recently I traveled for ten days throughout my native Kentucky. I visited the families of farmers, coal miners, and laid-off industrial workers. I spoke in tiny churches and drove on gravel roads dominated by overloaded coal trucks. I even meandered to the little community in Harlan County where I had been born. There I stood in the empty lots beside the Cumberland River where houses used to be: Becky Bailey's general store and post office, Polly Calwell's little yellow house with its porch that offered a grand view of the neighborhood's activities, my grandparents' house, destroyed by fire. Most of the houses have yielded to time, fire, or the so-called progress of the new road. The only familiar things now are the old church no one attends and the large cemetery no one leaves.

The day after I returned home, a friend said, "Tell me about your trip."

I shook my head. "I can't yet," I replied. "Every experience was a banquet; it will take me a while to sort it out."

For the next several days, I relived each adventure as

though pulling another layer from a mental onion. In time I could talk about my experiences, impressions, and reflections.

I think of that trip each time I read the comment in Luke 2:19 that Mary "pondered" events her heart. Truly, she needed time to sort everything out. She had been visited by an angel who told her that she was going to have a baby fathered by God; her betrothed husband had been convinced by an angel in a dream not to send her away in shame; she had given birth far from home, in a stable and without her mother and aunts to help; and then shepherds showed up at the stable, saying that a band of angels had told them where to find the newly born Messiah.

Mary's deeper understanding of all that had happened couldn't come overnight. She needed time to process the miraculous events and the wonderful part she, a simple country girl, had been chosen to play in those events. As I think about that not-so-ordinary teenager, I'm reminded that all of us sometimes need to take time to reflect on what God is doing in our lives. Her example inspires me with the thought that God, indeed, has a purpose for each of us—even this Harlan County, Kentucky, woman.

To Ponder:

Have you ever needed time to sort through events? If so, what was the situation?

What memories of an experience, person, or situation are you sorting through, perhaps years later? Which ones are the most difficult to share with others?

What types of emotions do you think Mary dealt with in her ponderings?

Dare to Be Silly

A cheerful heart is good medicine,
but a crushed spirit dries up the bones.
PROVERBS 17:22

Peggy's week in her blue-suit office world had been rough.
Now Saturday's chores loomed, it was raining, and both her
kids had colds. She pulled on her sweatshirt, then noticed she
had it on backward. She sighed and started to turn the logo to
the front.

Suddenly she grinned at her mirrored reflection and turned
her sweatpants inside out before she tugged them on. Then
she pulled her hair into a topknot and tied it with a pair of
her daughter's lavender tights. It was a "look."

Not only did she feel appropriately dressed for the gloomy
morning, but her attitude was brightened, too. And since then
she has learned to occasionally give in to other tension-
relieving "weird days." She's learned that sometimes we have
to force ourselves out of our ruts. Her sister, Darlene, learned
from Peggy's example and now takes her children for a daily
walk or, in bad weather, to the mall. Then she gives them
assignments to see how many different sounds or shades of a
particular color they can identify. The idea is to do something
different and something fun. But it begins with the determi-

nation to jump-start the creative part of the brain. Sure, it takes some effort, but Peggy and Darlene are evidence that the effort is worth it.

To Ponder:

Do you ever feel as though the daily grind is, well, grinding you down? What do you think you need?

Have you ever surprised yourself by doing something silly on a gloomy day? What happened?

What silly things would you like to try?

Passing Along a Chuckle

A happy heart makes the face cheerful.
PROVERBS 15:13

You've probably heard about endorphins—natural chemicals released by the brain when we laugh. I know their importance to health, but occasionally my life is so intense that I need an emotional "jump start" to get my endorphins rolling. That's when I remind myself of funny stories, including my favorite "You know it's going to be a bad day when . . ." jokes.

For example: You know it's going to be bad day when . . .

- your dentist is drilling, and you hear him mutter, "Oops."
- your car horn gets stuck as you're driving on the L.A. freeway—behind a group of Hell's Angels.
- your fourteen-year-old daughter mentions at breakfast, "Ya know, Jesus never preached against pierced noses."
- your four-year-old announces that it's *almost* impossible to flush a grapefruit.
- your neighbor announces that his sons' buddies will be over tonight, but don't worry, the music won't be too loud.

- your eight-year-old tells you the people down the street have new kittens they'll have to put to sleep if they don't get a new home.
- your grade-schooler mentions at bedtime, "Oh, Mom, I forget to tell you that I need a costume for the play tomorrow."

So how do *you* jump-start your chuckles? Endorphins are another reminder that we truly are "fearfully and wonderfully made." So go ahead—enjoy a good laugh.

To Ponder:

What helps when you need a good laugh?
What's your favorite joke?
Why do you think laughter is so important to our health?

Thankfulness through the Tears

I will give thanks to the Lord because of his righteousness.
PSALM 7:17

In 1981, Chet Bitterman Jr., a Wycliffe missionary in Bogota, Colombia, was kidnapped by rebel forces. As the world waited to learn the outcome, the young man's father furiously paced his Pennsylvania home, wondering how he could rescue his son. As he fumed, he felt the command within his heart, *Give thanks.*

To give thanks was the last thing Chet Sr. wanted to do. He'd already given serious thought to rounding up an armed group of his friends, flying into the South American city, and taking it apart, brick by brick.

But as he struggled with this new notion, he realized that the command was to *give* thanks, not *feel* thanks. Wondering what he could possibly be thankful for, he remembered that his son had memorized hundreds of Scripture verses.

Surely those verses are encouraging him right now, he thought. And he immediately gave thanks for the reassurance and courage the Word of God undoubtedly was giving his son at that very moment.

Upon further reflection, Chet Sr. added thankfulness for his son's physical strength and emotional stability. The list grew.

When young Chet's body was found in an abandoned bus forty-eight days later, those prayers of thankfulness allowed his father to open his heart to the comfort the Lord wanted to give him.

Remembering that account helped me face widowhood when my young husband died. I decided that if Chet Sr. could find something to be thankful for in the midst of his great emotional pain, surely I could, too. I could thank God for his reality, his help, his creative ideas, his untangling of the threads of my day.

Certainly I was grieving through the loss—as Mr. Bitterman grieved the loss of his son. To give thanks doesn't mean to deny pain. But it may well help us to bear it.

To Ponder:

Have you ever had a situation you were thankful in even though you weren't thankful for it?

What have you learned about thankfulness over the years?

What do you say to others who are struggling to be thankful in the midst of pain?

Fried Bear Meat

Give thanks in all circumstances, for this is
God's will for you in Christ Jesus.
1 THESSALONIANS 5:18

We've all had times of disappointment when God hasn't
given us what we've asked him for. But when I'm in those
situations, I try to remember the story of the old trapper who
got caught by a Colorado winter storm before he could gather
all of his provisions. As the blizzard raged and the cabin-
bound weeks wore on, the trapper's diet remained unvaried—
bear meat fried in bear grease.

One day, he prayed, "Lord, you know all I've had to eat for
days and days is this bear meat fried in bear grease. I don't
mind telling you I'm tired of it. Now, you've said that we're to
ask you to provide, so I'm trusting you to give me something
I can really enjoy as I sink my teeth into it."

The next day the man praised God for his special provi-
sion. Know what God had given him? Bear meat fried in bear
grease. *True, the situation hadn't changed, but his perspective*
had.

I like reminding myself of that story because I'm always
struggling with the way things "should be." But I'm also
finally catching on to the fact that this is not a perfect world,

and I'm not a perfect person. I'm even learning to relax and thank the Lord for what he *has* provided. And what a difference that makes.

To Ponder:

Can you identify with the old trapper? Why or why not? What things are you asking God to change in your life? What helps you wait for the answer?

Under His Wings

O Jerusalem, Jerusalem, you who kill the prophets and stone
those sent to you, how often I have longed to gather your
children together, as a hen gathers her chicks under her
wings, but you were not willing.

MATTHEW 23:37

When I was five years old, the chickens on our Kentucky
farm were important to us. They provided eggs for breakfast,
meat for supper, and feathers for the comforters stacked on
our mattresses. They were also a source of entertainment for
me as I watched their antics in the hen yard. Whenever a
storm darkened the sky over our fields, I loved to watch the
mother hens cluck to their chicks, calling for them to scurry
under their wings. Once each mother had her little brood
together, they would run to the safety of the henhouse.

In Matthew 23:37, Jesus uses this familiar image as he views
the city and cries out that he wanted to gather Jerusalem under
his protecting love in the same way a hen gathers her chicks.
This tenderness, emphasized in his repeating the city's name,
comes just after he had criticized the Pharisees for continuing
in their own hypocritical ways even as they were putting heavy
rules on others. Their self-righteous attitude so angered Jesus
that he called them "snakes" and "vipers."

Jesus also predicted that they would continue to kill those

sent to redeem them and warn of coming destruction to the city. But that prediction was barely out of his mouth before he poured out his lament that Jerusalem had ignored his love. In my imagination, I can see him stretching out his arms toward the city that housed the very ones who rejected him. Even then he was holding out his "wings," longing for the inhabitants to scurry to him.

I don't know about you, but I can have a tendency to over-look this aspect of our Lord—his sorrow when we ignore or, worse, turn from him. I can think of him as so all-powerful, so all-sufficient (which he is), that I forget his desire for me, for each of us, to come to him as his beloved child—and be sheltered under his eternal wings.

To Ponder:

What animal causes you to think of an attribute of the Lord?

What images of God's protection from Scripture are especially appealing to you?

Do you have a tendency to overlook some aspects of Jesus' character? If so, which ones?

Nothing in His Hands

You will receive a rich welcome into the eternal kingdom of
our Lord and Savior Jesus Christ.

2 PETER 1:11

When I used to call my parents back in Michigan, my dad
would often answer the phone from his favorite spot—the
garage. He'd be sharpening some tool, or changing the car's
oil, or organizing bolts and nails into the glass jars on top of
his workbench. He was an avid collector, too. He had a tool
collection, a license-plate collection, a political-button collection, a pocketknife collection.

Then as his health began to fail, he answered the phone
less from the garage and more from the house. One evening, I
tried to encourage him with talk of our beloved Kentucky.
"Now, Dad, you know that this next summer we're going to
start looking at places in the hills," I said. "You can have your
own cabin and be there anytime you want."

"I've got a better place than Kentucky to go to," he replied.

I hadn't grown up with him talking like that, so I didn't get
what he meant at first.

"Better than *Kentucky?*" I exclaimed. "What can be better
than Kentucky?"

He chuckled at my ignorance. "Why, heaven, honey!"

"Heaven?! Dad, we still need you *here*," I said. Then, trying to give my list-maker father something to look forward to, I added, "Now, I'm planning to fly out in a few weeks, so start thinking of things you want in a place to live. How close do you want to be to the road? Do you want a creek?"

We chatted for several more minutes, agreeing the new place had to have a big front porch where we could sit and listen to the whippoorwills "come a evening." I counted the days until my scheduled visit. Then the call came from my sister Thea, telling me that Dad's kidneys had begun to fail. Hospice had been called; the hospital bed had been delivered. Then she added that Jay, Holly, and I had better fly out.

There were reservations to be made, suitcases to be packed, a fitful night to get through, but the next morning, the three of us were on the first flight headed east to Michigan. However, by the time we arrived in early afternoon, Dad had already lapsed into semiconsciousness.

He squeezed my hand when I hurried to his bedside. Only then did I realize that the kitchen and living room were filled with relatives, quietly waiting. Someone pulled off my coat and steered me toward the chair at the head of the bed. I sat there throughout the rest of the day, talking to him, remembering our farm days together before economics had forced us north, reminding him of our visits back to the hills we both loved.

Gradually, his hand squeezes lost their strength and then finally stopped all together. He died a few hours later. Mother was on his right, holding his hand as he took the last raspy breath that escaped through his lips. All of us were silent—waiting, hoping for another breath. But it didn't come. And in that long moment, I looked at his big hands, hands that had tenderly wiped my tears on the farm, mended machines in the North, and rearranged his several collections. And then I realized that this avid collector of so many *things* was now touching the nail-scarred palms of his Savior—with nothing in his hands.

To Ponder:

What earthly possession do you most value?

What long-held dreams have you had to release because of the death of someone you love?

Has a loss ever given you a new perspective about possessions?

So *That's* What It Means!

Rejoice in the Lord always. I will say it again: Rejoice!
PHILIPPIANS 4:4

Have you ever misread a portion of Scripture or gleaned a wrong emphasis from a passage? For years as I read the Bible, I'd read Philippians 4:4 with the emphasis on only one word. I thought the verse said, *"Rejoice* in the Lord always. I will say it again: *Rejoice."*

Well, I had a long list of situations I couldn't get thrilled about, including several unfortunate childhood experiences, career struggles, and my husband's death from brain cancer at only thirty-nine. How could I rejoice?

But I finally started reading the verse in its entirety. It says, *"Rejoice in the Lord* always." Not in circumstances. Not in people. But in the *Lord.* That little insight makes a big difference. We don't have to rejoice over a tough life, but we can rejoice in the Lord's presence in the midst of the trials.

The morning before he died, Don, my beloved Scottish husband, said, "Just remember, San, the Lord never promised us an easy road. But he did promise to always be with us on that road."

What a wonderful promise. So now when I'm prone to

lament the bad things that happen, I don't berate myself for not rejoicing about them. Instead, I remind myself that I can choose, once again, to rejoice *in the Lord*—and thank him for his abiding presence.

To Ponder:

Have you ever misread a portion of Scripture? If so, how did new insight change your thinking?

Have you ever felt God walking with you on a difficult road?

In what ways have you had to rejoice in the Lord, rather than in your circumstances, during your life?

The Breathin' Part

He will wipe every tear from their eyes. There will be
no more death or mourning or crying or pain,
for the old order of things has passed away.
REVELATION 21:4

When my beloved Mama Farley died at age ninety, Don and
I decided that five-year-old Holly and six-year-old Jay would
attend the Kentucky funeral with us. During the long drive
south, we talked about heaven and told our children that
Mama—the part we couldn't see—was already with the Lord.
Then I, a veteran of southern funerals, told them about the
part they would see. She'd be lying in a big box, called a
casket, and surrounded by flowers. A lot of people would be
in the room, I said, and many would be crying because Mama
Farley couldn't talk to them anymore.

Then remembering previous funerals, I explained that some
people would touch her hands or kiss her forehead, often in
the belief such action would prevent bad dreams about the
person. We both stressed no one would make them kiss her,
but they could touch her hands if they wanted to.

I talked about the sad hymns the people would sing, what
the minister would do, and even about the procession to the
cemetery after her adult grandsons carried the casket to the big
car called a hearse. Then, most important of all, we asked if
they had any questions. Jay wondered about practical matters,

such as how they put the casket in the ground, but Holly just stared at me, her eyes round with silent wonderings.

When we arrived at the funeral home, we held the children's hands and walked into the flowered area. I studied Mama Farley's dear, ancient face and thought of the godly example she'd been throughout my childhood. I remembered the family unity during our farm days and longed for a skilletful of her incredible biscuits. And I thought of her faith-filled, pragmatic view of life. Still years away in my memories, I was startled by Holly's question:

"Is Mama breathing?" she whispered.

We hadn't anticipated that question. And it required more than just a quick "No, of course not." Suddenly this business of explaining death to myself had become difficult. How could I make a *child* grasp what I couldn't?

"Well, Holly . . . ," I stalled, searching for something both simple and theologically sound.

Jay then turned from flipping the casket handles to face his little sister. "No, Holly, she's not breathing. Remember? The breathin' part's in heaven."

Since that long-ago April day, I've stood before all too many caskets. But even with tears running down my cheeks, I find comfort in the memory of a little voice confidently announcing, "The breathin's part's in heaven." And that makes all the difference in being able to bear the grief.

To Ponder:

Has a child ever given you a different perspective about death? How so?

What is your earliest memory of someone special's death?

If you could tell a grieving relative only one thing about God's comfort, what would it be?

A PATCHWORK OF
WISDOM

Getting Rid of the Goat

He put a new song in my mouth,
a hymn of praise to our God.
PSALM 40:3

Have you ever felt as if life was piling on one problem after another, to the point where you felt adversity pressing in on all sides—and you longed for some emotional breathing space? There's an old rabbinical story I've found helpful in facing such "crowded conditions":

Housing was in short supply, so nine men were forced to live in one room, even though they weren't getting along very well. They called for their rabbi to settle their tensions. He looked at their glum faces and said, "I can solve your problem, but you must promise to do whatever I say. Agreed?"

The men glanced at each other and slowly nodded. The rabbi continued. "What you must do is get a goat to live here with you for one month," he said. "The problem will be solved after those thirty days."

Adding another creature to already crowded conditions wasn't the solution the men wanted, but they had given their promise. Reluctantly, they led one of the large goats from the nearby livestock pen and settled in for a long month.

Several weeks later, the rabbi saw one of the men on the street. "Well, how are things with all of you now?" he asked. The man beamed. "Oh, we're getting along great—now that the month is up and we've been able to get rid of the goat."

This favorite story got me thinking about some of the crowded conditions I've faced in my own life, such as growing up in a large family, sharing a small college dorm room with three other girls, and attending church retreats where several of us were required to share small rooms and tiny bathrooms. (I often joke that I became a retreat speaker so I could have my own room.) Beyond physical circumstances, there have been other times I felt I needed some emotional relief—to "get rid of the goat."

The tale of the goat vividly illustrates the importance of perspective. The truth is that there are many situations in life you and I can't change, however much we wish we could. But we *can* ask the Lord to help us develop a healthy perspective on that situation. And that may make all the difference in how we cope with our "crowded conditions."

To Ponder:

Have you ever felt physically or emotionally crowded? What was the situation?

Have you ever experienced the addition of a "goat" into an already difficult circumstance? If so, what happened?

What advice do you have for others who might find themselves overwhelmed by too many demands?

One Square Button

There are different kinds of gifts, but the same Spirit.
1 CORINTHIANS 12:4

I don't know about you, but I sometimes struggle with who I think I ought to be as a Christian woman. Shouldn't I be slim, silent, radiant, and, of course, able to play the piano? Well, I'm none of those things. But I'm learning—finally—to encourage myself with the delicious thought, *It's okay to be who I am.*

To remind myself of that point, I have on my desk a pint jar filled with antique buttons: tiny pearls from a baby's gown, coarse browns from a work shirt, bright blues from a Sunday dress, and my favorite, a bold red, green, and purple button that may have "fancied up" an otherwise drab winter coat.

I found the jar in an antique shop at a time when I was convinced I'd never fit the "proper woman" mold I felt others wanted me poured into. Actually, the jar I bought was positioned next to one with only boring white pearl buttons. But I ignored the pearl collection and purchased the jar filled with contrast and color—and less-than-perfect fasteners.

Now, whenever I get in one of my I'll-never-be-perfect

113

moods, I need only to look at my jar to be reminded life would be rather boring if we were all the same tiny pearl buttons. So if you're a bold red, green, and purple "button" like me who doesn't always fit in the pearl-button world, rejoice! All of us are needed—and fit—in God's perfect, interesting plan.

To Ponder:

Have you ever felt inadequate? If so, what was the situation?

What helps when you feel as though you can't accomplish all that's expected of you?

Describe the button you feel you would be most like.

What Jay and Holly Taught Me
about Communication

The lips of the righteous know what is fitting.
PROVERBS 10:32

Often when I speak at a retreat, young wives want me to provide a surefire way to get their husbands talking more. I remember my own early attempts to pull Don away from televised football games, so I can sympathize with those wanting more conversation. I had finally learned within my own marriage, however, that men and women tend to have different conversational styles and "different" doesn't mean "wrong"—as an incident with my teenagers a few years ago illustrated.

Three months after we moved to Colorado, Jay and Holly had flown back to see their New York friends perform in a play at their old high school. They flew out on the same morning, but because of their friends' schedules, they made arrangements to fly home on separate days.

I picked Holly up at the Denver airport on Wednesday. She got off the plane, hugged me, and started talking. She and Jay had attended our former New York church that past

Sunday, so I heard who had changed her hairstyle, who had gotten married, who was divorced, who was pregnant, who had delivered a baby, what the baby weighed at birth, what his name was, and what the mother dressed him in for church. I even heard about the pastor's tie. She talked— nonstop—for an hour and fifteen minutes! As we walked into our home, the phone was ringing. The call, of course, was for Holly.

The next day I went to the airport to pick up Jay. He got off the plane, hugged me, and said, "Everyone you ever met in New York says hi." End of discussion. He didn't say another word. He read all the way back to Colorado Springs.

So, having finally learned how different men's and women's conversational styles can be, I try to encourage young wives to stop expecting their husbands to respond the way a good female friend would. After all, we aren't going to change another person. All we can do is change our expecta-tions. And what a difference that attitude of acceptance makes in lowering our frustration level.

To Ponder:

Have you and someone of the opposite gender ever responded differently to the same situation? What happened?

Do you sometimes try to "fix" people, rather than accept their differences? How do they react to your efforts?

What have you learned about communication that you could pass along to others?

A Cliff-Hanging Lesson

Am I now trying to win the approval of men, or of God?
Or am I trying to please men?
GALATIANS 1:10

Do you expect that others will convey their appreciation for all you do? It's a hard lesson to swallow, but I learned not to get caught by that emotional trap years ago on a Kentucky mountainside.

Don and I had picked up my grandparents and my Aunt Adah to take them to Michigan for a visit with the relatives there. An all-day drive was ahead of us, so Mama had packed an enormous lunch and had it perched next to her on the front seat. On top of the picnic basket she had placed a large bunch of bananas before settling her cane comfortably against her thigh. She was ready for the trip.

Interstate 75 wasn't completed then, and numerous detours forced us to wind around the hills on dangerously curving stretches of asphalt. Topping one more hill, we discovered a rock slide covering the road. Don hastily set the gearshift in Park and got out of the car. Then he climbed onto a boulder to survey the situation. From my position in the backseat, I could see the steep ravine to our right that was filled with rocks. Beyond that were more incredible Appalachian mountains. As I smiled toward the view, the car slipped out of its gear and began to roll backward—toward the ravine! There was no guardrail.

I was wedged between Papa and Aunt Adah, but it was up to me to reach the brake. In that instant, I threw myself over the seat, knocking the lunch to the floor as I scrambled to stomp on the pedal. When I got the car stopped, we were already several feet beyond the asphalt and headed toward the five-hundred-foot drop.

With the car safely braked, I released my breath and tried to swallow my heart out of my throat. Then I looked at Mama, the one whose godly example and wisdom had so greatly influenced my entire life. Surely she had some praise for my quick action that had saved the four of us from severe injury—if not death.

But she merely glanced at me as she picked up the scattered lunch. Then she muttered, "You smashed the bananas."

Even now, whenever I'm tempted to expect praise for what I consider a spectacular feat, I remember Mama, bending over the damaged fruit. She hadn't seen the danger, so of course, she couldn't appreciate what I had done. I can accept that, but I confess I no longer like bananas.

To Ponder:

Have you ever felt unappreciated? If so, what was the situation?

When do you feel the most appreciated?

How do you show others you appreciate what they do?

Going to Plan B

*Do not conform any longer to the pattern of this world, but be
transformed by the renewing of your mind.*
ROMANS 12:2

Does your family have a Plan B for those times when your
preferred plan doesn't work out? We joke in this house that
we have so many things go wrong that we have Plans C, D,
E, and F. And some days, we even have to resort to Plan
"Triple Z."

But to remind me that the best things sometimes come
when my immediate plans don't work out, I have in my office
a pair of carved wooden, three-inch work boots. Their creator,
a Kentucky mountain man, had carved several of the little
pieces of footwear perfectly—and then the knife slipped. He
was almost finished on the one carved from buckeye wood,
but while turning the boot, he cut too deeply—and out
snapped the section holding the laces. He started to throw the
damaged carving into the fireplace but looked at it again with
new eyes. Picking up the broken piece, he whittled a little
mouse that he set inside the boot—just as though the creature
had eaten away part of the "leather." Then, with a grin, he
put a higher price on that item.

There are many situations that may not turn out exactly

the way we had planned. When this happens, we need to pray—but we also need to look with new eyes. God may just have something better for us, even if it's just a little carved mouse that adds unexpected beauty to a broken area of our life.

To Ponder:

Have you struggled with resolving a problem, only to suddenly see another, more creative alternative?

Do you institute backup plans for certain situations? If not, what happens when something doesn't pan out?

Do you have any tricks to spark your creativity?

The Message on a Closed Door

See, the former things have taken place,
and new things I declare.
ISAIAH 42:9

We've all heard the saying "When life hands you lemons, make lemonade." I've had to struggle with my teachers' frustration over my Kentucky accent, with job disappointment, and with many other difficult situations. But I've learned that good can come out of adversity—that there may be opportunities hidden behind closed doors. One of my favorite stories illustrates that thought:

The new boss at the office always left written instructions for the entire staff, including the evening cleaning crew. A janitor who could not read or write was fired when he failed to respond to the written messages.

But instead of giving in to discouragement, the man began his own cleaning business and eventually became very wealthy, even buying several buildings.

His banker was astounded when he discovered his prominent customer was illiterate. "Just imagine what you'd be if you could read and write!" he exclaimed.

The man smiled. "Yes, I'd still be the janitor in the building I now own."

Now this is not a pitch for illiteracy. Stories like this are rare. But the point is that what at first may look like failure may in fact be a hidden opportunity. We need to ask God to show us the message that may be written on a closed door—and when we learn to decipher it, another door just may open.

To Ponder:

Have you ever had a situation that was disappointing at first but turned out to be a good thing?

If you've had such a disappointment, what, if anything, would you have liked to have done differently?

What steps should folks take when they are faced with a major disappointment?

Pull Your Own Weeds

If a man will not work, he shall not eat.

2 THESSALONIANS 3:10

With delight I recall my years as the youngest member in a
four-generation Kentucky farm household. Our little community was filled with hard workers who prided themselves on
well-fed livestock, neat yards, and productive gardens. But
one farmer, whom I'll call Abraham, preferred sitting on his
porch to working his field. In the morning, he'd sit and watch
the sun rise above the gentle rolling hills around him. In the
evening, from his narrow back porch, he had a wonderful
view of the sun setting behind the ancient hickory trees that
lined his property. Each spring, in a burst of energy, he'd
plant a big garden but then neglect it, which resulted in a low
yield. It wasn't uncommon for his family to run short of food
before the next crop and have to ask for a few quarts of
canned vegetables from each of the neighbors.

Our family was one of those proverbial clans that used
every part of the butchered hog except the squeal—and if
we could have figured out a way to can that, it would have
been on the shelf, too. So my "waste not, want not" grandmother, Mama Farley, was growing increasingly frustrated

by Abraham's wastefulness. Finally, the day came when she finished the morning dishes early, replaced her work apron with her pretty "visiting" apron, and marched down the road to Abraham's house. As usual, he was sitting in a tipped-back chair as he casually whittled shavings from a small piece of red cedar.

"Well, good mornin', Miz Farley. What brings you over here today?" he asked.

Mama got right to the point. "Abraham, you've planted another fine garden, but it's going to weed—just like other years. You've got a family to take care of."

He barely looked up from his whittling. "Now, Miz Farley, the Lord always provides. All I have to do is pray."

Mama's eyes undoubtedly narrowed at that as she remembered how often her canned goods had made their way to his table, but she managed to stay calm.

"Well, Abraham, I tell you what," she finally said. "Why don't you try praying while you're out there in your garden pulling weeds?"

To Ponder:

Do you ever struggle with the line between how much is your part and how much is God's? If so, when?

What are some areas you have decided God has given you responsibility for? What areas are his responsibility?

Do you have any "Abrahams" in your life? How do you deal with them?

A Child's Prayer

For this God is our God for ever and ever;
he will be our guide even to the end.
PSALM 48:14

During the early weeks of our grief, I was determined that, while Jay and Holly had lost their dad physically, they weren't going to lose me emotionally. Every night as I tucked them into bed, I asked if they wanted to talk before we prayed together. Sometimes Jay shared a special memory of his dad or had a question about something at the funeral. But not eight-year-old Holly. She still hadn't cried and kept all of her searing questions inside. As she prayed, her words were rote instead of from the heart.

Each evening I continued to ask if she wanted to talk, but she'd shake her head and turn away. Then one night, about two weeks after the funeral, she paused, then said, "I do wonder one thing: When we prayed, didn't God listen?"

Oh, boy. With that one question, she'd galloped to the universal heart's cry.

Mentally I shot a quick prayer for calmness and fresh ideas as I began the hardest explanation I've ever tried to give: why it is that we can't compare the answer God gives us to the answer he gives someone else.

I reminded her of my Grandpa Ted, who had died after his leg was severed in a Kentucky coal mine. He had been only twenty-two years old and had left three children under the age of four. I reminded her of a twenty-eight-year-old man who had been killed at the corner just the week before. His wife was pregnant with a child he would never hold. Then I talked about God's gift to us of those extra sixteen months when the doctors thought her daddy would die within weeks. I added that he could have died with the first cancer when she had been only three years old.

When I was talked out, I asked if she felt like praying that night. She nodded, then began, "Thank you, God, that Daddy died now instead of when I was little."

I didn't hear much of the rest of her prayer.

To Ponder:

Have you ever had to talk to a child about the death of someone close? If so, what was the situation?

Have you ever wondered why God allowed someone you loved to die? If so, who was it?

How would you have answered Holly's question?

Got Any Other Bright Ideas?

The wisdom of the prudent is to give thought to their ways.
PROVERBS 14:8

Years ago, I drove Jay and Holly to school on a beautiful autumn morning. The Michigan sky was so magnificent I decided on the spur of the moment to leave the car in the school lot and walk home, do my housework, and then walk back to drive us all home that afternoon. All I had to do was stroll down the school driveway to Joy Road, turn right onto Lilly Road, and head home.

Then I surveyed the grassy field to my right. Hmm. If I cut across it, I'd get onto Lilly Road that much quicker—with only wet shoes from the dewy grass.

So I started off through the field, glorying in the beautiful morning. Soon my shoes and socks were indeed wet. The grass was deeper than I had thought, but it surely couldn't get any deeper—or so I told myself. I'd keep going.

After I went a few more feet, however, I realized the field had a gentle downhill slope. The grass that had looked only ankle-deep from the parking lot was now up to my knees.

I paused, considering the several yards of grass I still had to plow through before I'd be on the other side of the field—

and wondered if snakes ventured out this early. *Well, it can't get any worse,* I thought. *My shoes, socks, and slacks are already drenched. Might as well keep going.*

But less than a dozen steps farther on, the ground seemed to disappear and the grass was over my head! I slogged through the ravine, feeling as though I was fighting my way through the jungle in some B movie.

But I'd gone too far now to turn back. The worst was over. A few more steps and I'd be at the edge of the field and on Lilly Road.

By now I was soaked from head to toe with the heavy dew. But sure enough, as I plunged ahead, the grass was getting shorter again. It was at my waist, then at my knees, and finally just over my shoes. I was free!

But my rejoicing was short-lived. Just ahead was a deep, mud-filled gully. I stood there for several moments, looking at the muddy slope on the far side that would be impossible to climb, even if I could get down this side safely.

In a moment of wild, Tarzan-like fantasy, I even surveyed the large tree nearby, searching for a vine on which I could swing over to the other side. Nothing.

I looked back at the grassy field through which I had just come. I didn't want to claw my way through that again. *Surely I can climb this tree somehow and . . . no, they'll never find my body before spring.*

I could do nothing but turn around and go all the way back through that scary, wet grass. I finally arrived back at the car, which I drove home—I'd already had enough exercise for the morning—but I was in worse shape than if I'd taken the long way in the first place.

Hasn't that happened to all of us at one time or another? We plunge ahead with some ill-conceived plan, stubbornly ignoring the signs that point to disaster. Or we watch *some-*

one we care about heading for a tumble. Maybe if we all paused, prayed, and invited the Lord into our planning, we'd avoid those muddy "ditches" that lurk along the way.

To Ponder:

Have you ever been in a situation where you were convinced it couldn't get any worse—but it did? How did you cope?

What have been some of your greatest lessons from the "ditches" you've encountered in your own life?

Which camp are you in: "Forge ahead at all costs" or "Cut your losses"? Why?

When the Guilt Is Heavy

If we confess our sins, he is faithful and just and will forgive
us our sins and purify us from all unrighteousness.
1 JOHN 1:9

You may have learned, as I have, that a simple, heartfelt
apology offers emotional freedom. But what can you do when
the person to whom you need to apologize has died?

One of my friends, whom I'll call Joy, tells how stricken
she was when a widower in her church died. Just a few weeks
earlier she'd requested he postpone his frequent calls until
later in the evening: He had called several times just as she
was preparing dinner for her family. He never called again.

In the rush of her schedule, Joy forgot about him—until he
died. At the funeral home, his out-of-state daughter greeted
her with a hug, saying her father had commented about how
much it helped him to talk to Joy.

"After Mother died earlier this year, the dinner hour was
awful for him since he and Mother used to cook together and
catch up on the day's news," the daughter said. "You helped
him through a difficult time. Thank you so much."

Joy was too stunned, too embarrassed to confess, but the
next several days were rough for her as she replayed the
phone calls and her request that they stop. She gave herself

pep talks emphasizing how busy her large family kept her and how self-centered he had been to call during her busiest time of the day. The guilt remained.

Finally one evening, she knelt by her bed and said through her tears, "Lord, please tell him I'm sorry. I didn't realize what those calls meant to him, but if I could do it over again, I'd try to be more tuned in to what was really happening."

With that prayer, peace finally arrived—along with a new sensitivity to the hurting people around her.

To Ponder:

Have you ever allowed your busy schedule to overshadow your sensitivity to another's need? What was the situation?

How do you deal with feelings of guilt?

How do you try to be more sensitive to hurting people around you?

Loaves, Fishes and Corn Bread

Here is a boy with five small barley loaves and two small fish,
but how far will they go among so many?
JOHN 6:9

When a friend I'll call Mindy was a child, unexpected company often arrived at her family's modest home right at dinnertime. Her job was to stir up another batch of corn bread to stretch the meal as her mother greeted the guests. At the table, Mindy's mother would give her a wink that said, "Thanks for your help."

I think of that long-ago little girl whenever I read the John 6 account of a problem the disciples had that couldn't be solved with an extra batch of corn bread: five thousand men and their families had shown up unexpectedly for dinner! As Jesus watched the crowd approach (verse 6), he asked Philip where they could buy bread, but our Lord already knew what he was going to do. He was testing Philip, seeing how the disciple would deal with the situation. Philip, understandably, had no clue, exclaiming that even two-thirds of a man's yearly wages couldn't feed such a crowd!

In the midst of their discussion, Andrew stepped forward with a little boy who apparently had offered his own food.

But even as Andrew presented the gift, he questioned whether it would be enough.

Jesus didn't argue but gave Andrew instructions: "Have the people sit down." Then he took the bread and the fish, offered thanks, and began handing out the food.

Did the little boy's eyes grow wide as he watched his tiny lunch being multiplied? Did he wonder how Jesus did that? Was he delighted the Teacher used his gift to perform the miracle? I like to think maybe he just stood there grinning. And maybe Jesus winked his thanks.

I'd love to report that I identify with the little boy watching with awe as his meager meal was turned into an incredible banquet. Too often, though, my first response to many of life's crises is Philip's palms-up shrug. But gradually I'm learning that when I offer what little I can—like Mindy's corn bread and the little boy's lunch—then the Lord chooses to work. And many times, that understanding is the first miracle of the day.

To Ponder:

What is your usual first response to a challenge? What would you like your first response to be?

Have you ever been in a situation where you saw only the problem instead of a solution? What happened?

With which disciple in this account do you most identify?

A Gift to the Lord

There will always be poor people in the land. Therefore I
command you to be openhanded toward your brothers and
toward the poor and needy in your land.
DEUTERONOMY 15:11

One Saturday shortly after our daughter, Holly, was born,
we received a call from the church saying an unchurched
family needed furniture. They had bed frames and springs but
needed a mattress. Could we help?

We certainly could. In fact, we had just taken down our
guest bed to put up a crib for our newborn. The satiny white
mattress with the big blue flowers had been slept on only
twice and was now covered with blankets down in our basement. We were happy to have it put to good use again.

Don called the family to check on a convenient time for
delivery, and they agreed on three o'clock that afternoon.
Next, he called John, his buddy who owned a station wagon.
But when Don and John arrived at three o'clock, no one
answered their knock. Bewildered, they walked down the
steps to the vehicle, only to be met by a neighbor.

"Oh, they had stuff to do, but they asked me to watch for
you. They left a key; you can just bring the mattress in the
side door."

So Don and John pulled the mattress out of the station

wagon and lugged it into the house where the smell of cat urine and burned food hit their noses as soon as they opened the door. The neighbor gestured to the filthy wall across from the door and said, "They said just to leave it here. They'll take care of it later."

Don looked at the wall and battled his thoughts: *I can't believe how ungrateful these people are that they didn't stay around even after we agreed on the time. And now they want me to lean this spotless mattress against that filthy wall.*

Then in his heart, he said, *Lord, I can't give these people this mattress.*

He told me later it was almost as though the Lord answered, "Then give it to *me!*" and dropped a tangible peace around him.

Don nodded. *Okay, Lord. This mattress is yours, so if you want it left here, I guess that's your business.* And he and John leaned the mattress against the wall and left.

Neither of us could know it then, but his account of that delivery would stay with me long after his death and would, in fact, guide me as I faced my own times of giving things— and situations—to the Lord. And that's a pretty good lesson to learn from a slightly used mattress.

To Ponder:

Have you ever felt you were being asked to give to ungrateful folks? What was the situation?

How do you respond when you feel unappreciated? How would you like to respond?

What helps you differentiate between urgent needs and deeper needs?

What Will the Neighbors Think?

We are not trying to please men but God,
who tests our hearts.
1 THESSALONIANS 2:4

Do you struggle with what other folks think of you? I know I do. But it helps me to remember the ancient fable about the man who was caught in the same challenge. He and his son were on their way to market, leading the family donkey and enjoying the beautiful morning together.

One of their neighbors saw them and said, "Now isn't that silly? You have a fine donkey with you, but both of you are walking."

So the father put his son on the donkey, and they continued toward the market.

After a few minutes, another friend saw them and said to the son, "How rude you are to ride while your old father must walk."

So the child hopped off, and the father climbed onto the donkey's back. It wasn't long, however, before they met another neighbor who said to the father, "That's terrible that you, a grown man, are riding while this poor child must walk."

So the father pulled his son up in front of him on the

donkey's back, and they continued on toward town, enjoying the beautiful morning.

Of course, you know what happened next. Yes, another neighbor saw them and exclaimed, "Oh, that poor donkey! How terrible you both are riding on his little back."

So the father and his son slid off the donkey, and the strong father picked up the bewildered animal and slung it across his shoulders. Together, he and his son continued toward town. Just as they rounded another corner, though, they met another neighbor, who looked at them in disgust.

"Well, if that isn't the stupidest thing I've ever seen," he exclaimed. "Donkeys are to be ridden, not carried!"

You and I can't please everyone, no matter what great lengths we go to. So let's set our goal on pleasing the Lord.

To Ponder:

Have you experienced a situation where your effort produced repeated criticism? What happened?

What struggles do you still confront as you try to please others?

What advice do you have for others who face criticism?

Accepting the Consequences

Discipline your [child], for in that there is hope.
PROVERBS 19:18

One afternoon when Peg's son, Charles, was three, she gave him a frozen treat, which he licked and then waved about before taking the next bite.

"Don't wave it around like that, honey," she said. "It will fall off the stick. If it falls off, I won't give you another one."

But of course, he didn't listen, and sure enough, the frozen orange treat fell onto the grass. Immediately he turned to her and demanded another one.

"No, honey," she replied. "I'm sorry, but that's what happens when you aren't careful."

Maybe you're thinking, *Oh, come on. That's a little extreme.* Okay, perhaps. But when do we as parents start to teach our children that actions have consequences? It's better, I'm convinced, to teach that important lesson while the consequences of the child's actions are less severe.

I'm reminded of how God deals with us, his mistake-prone children. It always amazes me how much responsibility he gives us, how much freedom—because he knows that we will never learn, never grow, if he doesn't allow us to make mistakes and experience the consequences.

Sure, we could step in and shelter our kids from the results of their mistakes. Our Father could step in and do that for us. But he chooses not to—and as we struggle with our freedom, we often learn a deeper trust and dependence on the Lord.

To Ponder:

At what age do you think children should be taught to accept the consequences of their actions?

At what age did you start learning that actions have consequences?

How do you think parents can best teach this important lesson?

Demanding Perfection

Her husband has full confidence in her. . . . She brings him
good, not harm, all the days of her life.
PROVERBS 31:11-12

My fiftieth birthday suddenly—and officially—thrust me into
the role of an "older woman of the church." I found that
many of the young women around me were asking for advice
about careers, long-distance moves, and even love. I remember one intense young woman—I'll call her Mallory—who
longed to be married, but none of the men she dated could
live up to her high demands. If a young man planned an
event several weeks in advance, she wanted him to be more
spontaneous. If another called at the last minute for coffee,
she was irritated he hadn't been more courteous and planned
ahead. She was particular about how her dates dressed, even
declining a second date when her escort showed up with a
shirt she thought clashed with his trousers. If her dates talked
about sports, she was bored. If they talked about their work,
she said they were self-absorbed.

Well, you get the picture. Even in her human *imperfection,*
she was looking for *perfection.* And she hadn't yet learned
that she was not going to find it.

Sometimes we women have a tendency to place too many

141

perfectionistic demands on other people, including the men in our lives. Perhaps we need to consider what Jim Elliot, a martyred missionary, thought about such demands. He said, "A wife—if she is very generous—may allow that her husband lives up to perhaps 80 percent of her expectations. There is always the other 20 percent that she would like to change, and she may chip away at it for the whole of their married life without reducing it by very much. She may, on the other hand, simply decide to enjoy the 80 percent, and both of them will be happy."

Hmmm. I wonder what would happen if we adopted such an attitude in all our day-to-day relationships?

To Ponder:

Do you ever wonder if your high expectations of others interfere with some of your relationships?
What do you think about Jim Elliot's comments?
What do you see as some of the greatest barriers in developing friendships?

Playing with Snakes

A man's own folly ruins his life.
PROVERBS 19:3

When Holly was in her late teens, I was concerned about a young man she was dating. I confess I was relieved when they broke up, especially since she began to spend more time with her friends from church.

Then one night, Holly was on the phone as I went into her room to say good night. I gestured a gentle "Cut it short," then went to my room and gratefully pulled the quilts around my shoulders. I fell into a deep sleep but had the most disturbing dream of Holly picking up snakes from her floor. She'd hold them up, examine them, and let them writhe over her hands.

Ugh! I woke up, my heart pounding from the vividness of the dream. I looked down the hallway and could see a light from under her door, even though it was almost midnight.

I found her still on the phone and motioned for her to sign off. Then I sat on the bed and asked why she was still up. She explained that her old boyfriend had called.

Suddenly my nightmare made sense. I told her about it, then added, "Holly, be careful whom you date. Don't play with snakes."

She didn't date that young man again, and that phrase has now become one of our family codes to remind us to stay out of situations that are potentially harmful. (Something positive came out of that awful dream after all.)

From time to time, we all—no matter what our age—need to remember that there are "snakes" out there, people and situations that could harm us. God's Word is clear on that. But his Word is also clear that, armed with wisdom, prayer, and confidence in the Lord, we can recognize—and walk away from—those snakes when they invite us to play with them.

To Ponder:

Have you ever deliberately headed toward a potentially harmful situation? What happened?

Has a timely warning ever kept you from a bad decision?

What do you say when you want to warn someone against a particular decision or relationship?

On a Street in Old Jerusalem

Whatever you did for one of the least
of these . . . you did for me.
MATTHEW 25:40

Just in front of the slabs of lamb in the open-air meat market in Old Jerusalem, I saw a young Palestinian mother. Cradled in her left arm was a baby. With her right hand, she was steering a little boy about three years old. Even though her long gray-green dress and white head scarf announced her different culture, I thought of my own days of juggling two babies and several purchases.

Just then a collective groan went up as the people around me began moving to the sides of the narrow, covered street. That's when I saw the garbage tractor inching toward us. The streets were already crowded; how could the driver get that tractor through here?

But still I moved aside with the crowd, muttering my usual "Sorry" to uncomprehending ears. The tractor advanced upon us, forcing us to flatten ourselves—four deep on each side— against the storefronts and each other. Slowly, the machine began to crawl past us, its oversized tires only millimeters from my back.

Suddenly someone was pummeling my legs. I looked down to see that the little son of the Palestinian mother was trying to fight his way past me—and into the path of those fearsome tires.

145

I grabbed his shoulder and looked beyond the tractor to where I had last seen the young mother, knowing the panic she must feel. She also was trapped in the mob, clutching the baby close to her face to keep the child from being crushed. But while she was protecting the one, her eyes were darting over the crowd for the other who had been separated from her in the pushing.

Still gripping her little son's shoulder with one hand, I waved to her with the other while her little boy kicked my ankles for all he was worth.

"He's here. I have him!" I shouted to her.

Her bewildered stare let me know she didn't understand me, and all of us were pressed too tightly together for me to pick the child up for her to see. All I could do was point dramatically at my feet and nod encouragingly, hoping she understood that her son was safe.

At last, the monstrous tractor passed, and I could steer the child to his anxious mother. As he recognized her skirt, he clutched it, crying with relief. I touched his dark hair and looked into the brown, misty eyes of his mother as she nodded her thanks to me.

I wanted to tell her about my own two children. But I couldn't speak her language, so we simply gazed at one another. I touched her little boy's head once more and then slipped back into the throng of shoppers.

To Ponder:

What could you do for a child outside your immediate family?

Has anyone ever ministered to your child in a meaningful way? How did you express your appreciation?

What do parents of all cultures share?

WORKDAYS, HOLIDAYS,
AND EVERY DAYS

So You Goofed

*Be kind and compassionate to one another, forgiving each
other, just as in Christ God forgave you.*

EPHESIANS 4:32

Years ago, I made a bad mistake in ordering for my department in a major organization. In the midst of my panic, I
asked myself, *Wait—what's the worst that could happen
because of this?*

Well, I could get fired, was my immediate thought.

I was confident no one was going to ship me to Siberia
(even though the thought may have crossed a few minds)—but
I knew I needed to fix the situation. So instead of continuing
to wring my hands, I started working like crazy to get the
problem straightened out. I breathed a prayer and went to
the department head to confess. Inwardly trembling, I fully
expected him to yell at me. Instead, he understood the lack
of communication I'd gotten caught in and told me which
department could help me.

Then, rather than telling me how stupid I was (I already
knew that), he smiled and said, "This is not the worst thing
we've had happen here, you know."

Well, I *hadn't* known that, and he was kind to point it out.
Later, I was still so astonished by his quiet, professional

response that I began to analyze my own reactions to others. How many times had my panic increased another's trauma? How often had I ignored an opportunity to bring peace to an emotional storm? Those reflections gave me something to think about—and work on.

To Ponder:

Have you ever made a major mistake at work? What was your first reaction?

Have you ever asked yourself, What's the worst that can happen? Did the answer help or send you into panic?

How do you respond when others make mistakes around you? What is your desired response?

How to Erase Your Tapes

Being confident of this, that he who began a good work in you
will carry it on to completion until the day of Christ Jesus.
PHILIPPIANS 1:6

Margo felt as though she were drowning in her new job.
And her self-talk wasn't helping one bit as she'd mutter, "I'll
never figure out this computer program. What made me think
I could ever do this?" She played those mental tapes so much
that she finally convinced herself that she had no option
other than to quit.

We may think, *How sad.* Maybe we even wonder why she
didn't talk to her supervisor about tutoring or why she didn't
take a computer class at the community college. But don't we
play similar mental tapes when we're facing an emotional
mountain? Or perhaps we're still replaying those memories of
a drunken parent's lament for producing us or perhaps a
former teacher's critical assessment of our skills.

It's hard to erase those old tapes, even though we know
they paralyze us emotionally and cripple us with defeatist
attitudes. What I've tried to do is replace those old negative
messages with encouraging thoughts. For example:

God didn't bring me this far to leave me alone.

I can *do this.*

This, too, shall pass.

And my feisty favorite: *Keep hanging on to the Lord and don't let the "turkeys" win!*

To Ponder:

What mental tapes do you play when you're struggling with a situation?

What do you find most helpful when you want to beat up on yourself emotionally?

How have your mental tapes changed over the years?

Fighting for My Wrinkles

Even to your old age and gray hairs I am he, I am he who will
sustain you. I have made you and I will carry you; I will
sustain you and I will rescue you.
ISAIAH 46:4

When I look into the mirror, I see a Titus 2:4 woman, someone who has the privilege of encouraging and teaching younger women.

Do I miss the smooth skin of my youth? Of course. But do I mourn its loss? No—each line represents another milestone in my journey toward becoming the woman God wants me to be.

Recently, I had my annual publicity photo taken by a local studio. Since the prints were simple black-and-white, head-and-shoulders shots, I expected them back within a few days. But when I called, the photographer's assistant said I couldn't have them for another week; she'd sent them to the finishing department to have the lines around my eyes airbrushed out.

"I don't want those lines brushed out," I said. "I've worked hard for them."

"But," she pointed out unnecessarily, "they make you look middle-aged."

"I *am* middle-aged," I declared. "Leave my wrinkles alone."

I refused to give in, and the photos were ready for pickup

that afternoon. And, clearly, the wrinkles of years past were all there, unretouched and undiminished by cosmetic artifice. But those same lines are also evidences of a relaxed and even joyful attitude as I look forward to the adventures and fulfilling experiences that—as the Lord allows—await me in the years ahead.

To Ponder:

What's your attitude toward growing older?

What do you think is one of the most difficult aspects of aging?

Who has given you a good example of "growing old gracefully"?

Working Hands and Strong Prayers

[She] is well known for her good deeds,
such as bringing up children, showing hospitality,
washing the feet of the saints, helping those in trouble
and devoting herself to all kinds of good deeds.
1 TIMOTHY 5:10

Every time I read Paul's instructions to Timothy about the elderly widow's place in the church, I think of my Kentucky grandmother, Mama Farley. She lived out the role Paul described: Her reputation in her coal-mining community was impeccable, and her neighbors knew she could be counted on in any crisis to supply food, working hands, and strong prayers. Every visiting preacher stayed with her family. Her handmade quilts would be prizewinners today. Unemployed men on their way to look for a better way of life during the Great Depression often wound up at her family's table, where she heaped the produce of her garden onto their plates while reminding them that the Lord had not forgotten them. In fact, one 1939 afternoon, she stepped into her garden just as a weary hitchhiker bit into a plump yellow tomato he had pulled from the vine. Mama watched the juice run down the man's chin, then quietly said, "Now you come on into the house. That'll taste better with the chicken and dumplings left over from dinner." And the man gratefully followed.

But despite all of Mama's abilities, if you were to have

asked her what one thing she had accomplished, she wouldn't hesitate: "Raising my family."

Paul's first letter to Timothy includes child rearing with the other important aspects of being a woman of God. Unfortunately, in today's society, the value of that task isn't always held in great esteem. But what greater accomplishment can one have than to make a difference in another's life—beginning with the children placed in your care? Child rearing not only has God's blessing upon it but actually helps proclaim his reality. Mama Farley understood that, and her daylong conversations with the Lord as she went about her work emphasized the priority she placed on family: *Now, Lord, thank you that you're with all my young'uns right now—at school and at work. Keep 'em from harm, Lord. Tell the enemy he can't have 'em, and help each one to grow to serve you.*

Whether she was hoeing the garden, canning the produce, tending a sick neighbor, or cooking another one of her country suppers, she never saw her care for her family as a waste of her talents, but rather as an opportunity to use her skills. And as her husband and eight children returned home each evening, she would pull the hot corn bread out of the woodstove and whisper thanks for her heavenly Father's care throughout another day.

To Ponder:

Who in your life reminds you of the widows Paul talked about in his letter to Timothy?

What are some of the qualities you admire in godly older women?

What godly qualities are you striving for?

Bottle Rockets

You need to persevere so that when you have done the will of
God, you will receive what he has promised.
HEBREWS 10:36

I learned how tightly people cling to what's safe and familiar
the year I tried to take my kids to an honest-to-goodness fireworks show.

We had always spent the Fourth of July at the lakeshore,
where they were contented with backyard sparklers. The year
came, though, when I decided to introduce Jay, ten, and
Holly, nine, to a big-league display. In the middle of the
afternoon, however, Jay bounded into the house.

"Mom! Guess what! The kids down the street are gonna set
off bottle rockets as soon as it gets dark."

I looked up from my mending. "Remember, honey, we're
going to the park. We won't be here."

Jay frowned. "Aw, Mom. I don't wanna go."

"Honey, you've never seen real fireworks. You'll love 'em!"

His frown deepened. "It's not fair you're making me go."

I was amazed at his balking, and for the next few minutes
we argued. Finally, I stood up. "Jay, that's enough. I'm pulling rank; you *are* going to join me and Holly tonight."

He turned away, thoroughly disgusted. At supper and again

during the drive to the park, he ignored me. Shortly, we found a spot in the midst of the crowd and spread out the blanket. Then I opened the picnic basket.

"What do you want? Juice or a cola?" I asked. Holly chose the juice. I held the lid open, waiting for Jay's choice and wondering if he'd refuse rather than have to answer me. He mumbled, "Cola." I tried not to grin as I handed him the drink.

While we waited for darkness, I chatted about the displays I had attended as a child. Only Holly appeared to be listening.

At last the test rocket went up, its thin gray smoke trailing out against the sky. Then came the harsh whistle of the real rockets, followed by an orange explosion. The brilliant sphere hung over our heads, enticing a collective "ahhh" from the crowd. Both Jay and Holly tipped their heads back, their eyes wide with delight. Suddenly Jay turned to me.

"Wow, Mom, this is great!"

I bit my tongue to keep from saying, "I *told* you."

Another rocket went off just then, sending showers of red and green across the sky. For the next thirty minutes we gawked at two-stage releases, impressive tricolors, "squigglers," and at last, the dazzling finale. As we left the park, Jay was back to his talkative self.

That night I thought of past quarrels with my own parents. Those memories quickly moved on to the times I had argued with my heavenly Father, convinced my way was better than his. When I went to bed that night, I filed the situation away as a handy spiritual lesson. . . .

Three years later, a marvelous job opportunity came. Unfortunately, it was 650 miles away. Surely I couldn't leave my familiar small town for a suburb of New York City. How could I uproot my children from all they had known? What about my friends? My job? My comfortable home?

In prayer I struggled—wanting to accept the new challenge but not wanting to break away from the familiar. Finally in exasperation, I confessed aloud what the Lord already knew.

"Oh, I just want to stay here!"

Immediately, a thought popped into my mind: *and shoot bottle rockets?*

A sigh accompanied my surrender. "All right, Lord. I trust the unknown to you."

We moved in record time, and despite the typical adjustments, we found our niche in new surroundings. Best of all, I so enjoyed the new challenges that at times I was tempted to give a most unprofessional squeal: "Wow, Lord, I'm glad I didn't choose bottle rockets over this!"

And I'm sure he smiled.

To Ponder:

Have you ever balked at—and later thanked the Lord for—
something he invited you to do? What was the situation?
What's the hardest part of change for you?
What advice would you give someone who is afraid of a
new challenge?

Quilts on the Walls

She makes coverings for her bed;
she is clothed in fine linen and purple.
PROVERBS 31:22

Are you one of those people who has to have things "just so"? I used to be. But when I was offered an editorial position with a Christian magazine in the New York City area and we moved into a small condo, the cost of living was so high on the East Coast I couldn't afford wallpaper right away. So we slapped paint on the walls and moved in.

Within a couple of days of unpacking our boxes, I had hung—with dozens of straight pins—several Amish and southern quilts to add brightness to the rooms. Then on the awkward wall next to the stairs leading to the second floor, I hung the rag rugs my Kentucky grandmother had braided years ago. Only a few of them looked new; most were the ones I had wiped my feet on at her back door years ago, never dreaming they would someday move with me to that great end of the world—New York.

When everything was in place, I stood back to admire the splashes of color against the off-white paint. It was magnificent! What I had originally meant as a temporary measure quickly became my personal decorating signature, and every home I've had since then features those same wonderful quilts.

I think most of us struggle from time to time with discontent over the way our house looks. But you know what? What makes a house attractive and inviting is your personality reflected in the house—a collection that has meaning to you, some much-loved books, the table you picked up at a flea market as a newlywed. Houses like that say, "Welcome—real people live here!" and are better than sterile perfection any day.

To Ponder:

How do you deal with anxiety about how your house looks? What, if anything, has helped you?

Can you recall a time when "necessity was the mother of invention" when you were decorating or furnishing your house?

What items in your home best announce your personality?

Plant Your Own Garden

He makes me lie down in green pastures,
he leads me beside quiet waters.
PSALM 23:2

As I approached my third year of widowhood, well-meaning friends asked me when I was planning to start dating and get remarried. I laughingly said I didn't have room in my busy life—nor my cluttered closet—for a second husband. Then I added I wouldn't even think about that prospect until someone showed up with a dozen roses. Then I changed the subject.

That evening I mentally replayed the conversation and—knowing I often veil the truth with my humor—asked myself a tough question: *Would I really be attracted to the first guy who handed me roses?*

Well, as I admitted that he would at least get my attention, I made an important decision: *Plant my own garden.*

The next morning, I was at our local gardening shop loading my car trunk with fifteen rosebushes and several bags of peat moss. For the next three months, I pruned and sprayed—and kept fresh roses throughout the house, quietly marveling at the self-satisfaction I gained from the bright, fragrant blooms.

Not long after that, I began "planting my own garden" in other areas of my life as well, taking the first steps that led me to a new career. If I had waited for someone else to bring me roses—and to "rescue" me from my single state—I would have missed changing careers and taking the incredible adventure that has been my life for the past several years.

So how about you? Are you waiting for someone else to show up with life's "roses"? Are you putting off taking a special trip or buying good china or replacing the lopsided chair? Are you putting your life on hold instead of taking action? What's keeping you from planting your own garden?

To Ponder:

Have you ever put your life on hold, waiting for someone else to make a decision or take action? If so, what was the situation?

If you've ever put your life on hold because of someone else, what would you do differently now if you could?

What advice do you have for others who may be in the same emotional boat?

A New Thanksgiving

For whoever wants to save his life will lose it,
but whoever loses his life for me will find it.
MATTHEW 16:25

Are you approaching the first holiday without a loved one?
Those times can be tough, but you *can* get through them. I
remember the first Thanksgiving after my husband, Don, died.
His favorite meal always had been the traditional holiday
dinner. He'd invite all the relatives, and I'd cook. We always
had a twenty-two-pound turkey with dressing, gravy, two
kinds of potatoes, four vegetables, hot rolls, and pies—oh,
those pies. But I didn't want to cook dinner if he wasn't there
to say, "Great meal, San."

However, for the sake of our children, I couldn't give in to
depression and spend the day in bed, either. Several of our
friends, bless 'em, had invited us for dinner, but spending the
day with someone else's "perfect family" was just going to
make my loss all the more vivid. I knew I had to get my eyes
off myself, so I called the Salvation Army and offered that the
three of us would work. That was exactly the right decision:
two minutes of watching other single mothers, street people,
the elderly, and even traditional families come for dinner in
that little hall showed me another world—and put my own
grief in perspective.

I blinked back tears as I watched folks arrive that day. What had they lost? What about the smiling lady in the thin cotton dress? Had she once cooked for a large family? Perhaps her husband had squeezed her shoulders and whispered, "Great meal, hon." Or what about that man in the shiny suit? Did he live in one of the lonely downtown hotels? Had he come for the company as well as the meal?

As I heaped food on sturdy paper plates instead of my blue-and-white china, I gradually saw my own problems in a different light. We *do* help ourselves as we help others—or, as Jesus put it, we find our life through losing it.

On that Thanksgiving Day, I was grateful after all.

To Ponder:

Have you experienced a first holiday without a loved one? If so, how did you get through the day?

Why are the holidays often more difficult to get through than ordinary days after a death or divorce?

What advice do you have for those who are approaching that first lonely holiday?

The "Perfect" Holiday

Thanks be to God for his indescribable gift!
2 CORINTHIANS 9:15

Years ago, the arrival of red-and-green store displays would plunge me into a marathon of baking, gift making, and decorating. I just had to match the scenes created in those *Best Holiday Ever!* women's magazines.

So I fussed over making clothespin angels and gingerbread villages—and wondered why my children didn't appreciate the magic I slaved to make for them. Finally, one winter evening in the midst of my holiday planning, I realized I had been trying to match scenes created by a magazine staff of twelve. Armed with that insight, I asked my then-young teens, Jay and Holly, for ways we could tame our holiday schedule.

Youngsters have wonderful imaginations, so they reeled off suggestion after suggestion, including ways they could get creative with their own gift giving to their friends. Jay, in fact, came up with a masculine version of Christmas baking: huge cookies, baked individually on a pizza pan, then wrapped in a food-storage bag, tied with a red bow. Even he was surprised at what a big hit they were, especially with the girls in his class, who were impressed that he could bake.

The three of us have learned a lot since those early years when I tried to outdo the seasonal magazines. Oh, I'll never create the perfect Christmas setting that still exists in my head, but by remembering the One whose birthday we're celebrating, I can create the perfect Christmas in my heart. And that is a gift to cherish.

To Ponder:

Have you ever been caught in the magazine image of the perfect Christmas?

Are you happy with the way you prepare for the holidays? If so, what's your secret? If not, what would you like to change?

What special holiday activities are too important to you and your family to ever change?

The Warmest Gift

Give, and it will be given to you.
LUKE 6:38

As the first Christmas after my husband's death loomed, I called the Salvation Army and offered that my children and I would deliver food baskets to the elderly or ill. The staff welcomed our help, but the morning of our assignment was so bitterly cold that I couldn't get warm even with my new coat tightly buttoned against the wind.

Still, I had promised, so the three of us made deliveries up rickety steps to above-the-store apartments and weather-beaten houses near the railroad tracks. We carried in the bags of food and offered a hearty "Merry Christmas" along with each good-bye, but the cold continued to penetrate my coat—and my heart. I was cold, the weather was miserable, and I couldn't see that I was making a great difference in anyone's life. After all, if we hadn't been delivering the groceries, someone else would have.

Then we arrived at the last tired little house, where we were invited in. Everything was clean, but the floor covering was worn down to the wooden boards. Only near the walls were pieces of ancient tile. The curtains had been mended so

169

many times the stitches made a pattern in the thin material. As I set down the bag containing a small turkey, potatoes, green beans, cranberry sauce, and rolls, the couple in their late seventies thanked me repeatedly. All I had to do was smile and walk out the door, but there was a wistfulness in their voices as they invited us to "stay awhile." So we remained for a brief, delightful visit, and upon discovering the woman's need for a coat, I gave her mine.

She hugged me as she accepted and whispered, "God bless you, honey," as tears rolled down her cheeks. All I could do was whisper back, "Thank you for letting me do this."

When my children and I left, we waved to the couple. Then Holly turned to me. "Mom! It's freezing out here! And you gave away your coat!"

I gave her shoulders a little squeeze. "I know. But this is the warmest I've been all day—in fact, the warmest I've been in a very long time."

She gave me a bewildered look, and we climbed into our car to head for home.

To Ponder:

Have you ever tried to fend off depression by helping others? What happened?

Has your gift ever appeared to others to be a sacrifice, but actually you were the one helped in the giving? If so, what was the situation?

What would you like to do differently in gift giving?

The Thirty-Four-Dollar Christmas

*He has scattered abroad his gifts to the poor, his
righteousness endures forever.*

PSALM 112:9

When my adult children and I talk about Christmas now,
our conversation always gets around to the year our move
from New York to Colorado resulted in our having only
thirty-four dollars to spend for gifts. Our new friends in the
area were mostly other single parents and their kids, and we'd
planned to all gather at our home Christmas Day. So a few
weeks before the holiday, I explained our financial crunch,
without embarrassment, then suggested we exchange homemade items or gifts of service at the dinner. The other parents,
who were also struggling that year, were relieved at my
suggestion. We agreed we'd see this as an adventure rather
than "belt-tightening."

Christmas morning arrived. Our personal family time began
with our own gift exchange in which Jay gave his sister
coupons redeemable for his help with her math homework.
Holly, in turn, gave him coupons promising to do several
loads of his laundry.

Jay's gift to me was a pack of coupons for eight long
evening walks together. Holly's gift was a free-verse poem

171

called "Parenting," in which she thanked me for being a "great person and mom." Of course I cried when I read it.

A few hours later, the other families arrived for a potluck dinner. When it was time to open gifts, we exchanged promises for help with errands, plates of homemade cookies, and creative gifts, including spray-painted avocado candlesticks. It was an incredible day—and all because we didn't allow a lack of money to spoil our fun.

So what can you do to make the next Christmas memorable? Remember that the best Christmases don't come from charge cards and piles of gifts, but from finding new ways to reach out to others as you celebrate the reason behind this holiday—the birth of Jesus.

To Ponder:

Which Christmas celebrations stick out in your memory? Why?

Have you ever been forced to be creative for a particular Christmas? What happened?

What suggestions do you have for those who feel Christmas isn't fun unless a mountain of gifts is under the tree?

Watching for God's Touch

*I watch in hope for the Lord, I wait for God my Savior; my
God will hear me.*

MICAH 7:7

What's your favorite New Year's Day activity? Some folks
watch football, visit relatives, eat a special food, or take down
the Christmas tree. My January 1 activities may vary from
year to year depending on the wishes of my visitors, but I
have one important annual ritual: I open the new calendar
and list all the special birthdays and anniversaries for the
coming year. Then I turn to each month, plop my finger on
a random date, and write the command "Watch for God's
Touch" in the space.

Then, as those particular days arrive throughout the year,
I watch for ways in which God reminds me of his presence.
Sometimes his special touch comes through a new insight
into a Scripture verse, an encouraging phone call or letter,
perhaps an unexpected and much-needed rebate check, or a
Rocky Mountain double rainbow. Sometimes nothing
dramatic at all occurs, but I have a fresh awareness of God's
presence—and all because I was watching for it. And once
I started looking for God's touch on specific days, I found
myself aware of it on ordinary days as well.

How about you? Do you need God's touch on *your* day? Maybe all you have to do is start watching for it.

To Ponder:

When are you most aware of God's presence?
In what way do you bring him into your day-to-day life?
Have you developed any "rituals" to help you watch for God's touch?

COURAGE

The Many Faces of Courage

Do not be terrified; do not be discouraged, for the Lord your
God will be with you wherever you go.
JOSHUA 1:9

In my final year of college, I worked as a civilian secretary
for an ROTC unit during the Vietnam War. In addition to my
usual clerical duties, I had the opportunity to view several
aspects of the future soldiers' jungle survival training, including one ranger's demonstration of skinning a snake without a
weapon!

Since I was surrounded with military examples, I decided
that courage was best demonstrated by fresh-faced young
men rushing into battle. Then after the war ended, a local
nursing home burned, and several firemen risked their lives
to save the elderly patients. I added them to my list of those
I saw as models of courage. Next, I heard stories of martyred
South American pastors who refused to deny their faith even
when challenged by rebel soldiers. My list grew and continued to grow. But always it consisted of folks whose courage
was public.

Then my husband was diagnosed with metastatic brain
cancer, and the doctors were saying he would have as little as
two weeks to live—or as "long" as three months. Suddenly I

had a new example of courage: Don, who was determined not to let the doctors bury him yet. I watched him grab each day's joy, and I marveled that he could face death with such quiet courage.

Now all these years later, I've had numerous opportunities to ponder courage. Sometimes I think of Don's smile during his illness or Aunt Adah's gentle acceptance of a debilitating and progressive brain disease. Sometimes I think of people who left the familiar to start new lives—like my parents, who became part of the Great Migration from the South to the North in the early 1950s; or missionary friends, who moved to a foreign country; or my dear Canadian daughter-in-law, who moved to the U.S. Sometimes the courageous face before me is a stroke or accident victim who decides to adjust to her disability. Sometimes I see single parents who climb over great obstacles to care for their children. Sometimes bravery comes in the form of a woman who carries to term the child others suggested she abort.

Through the years, I have learned that courage doesn't always mean rushing into battle. Often it calls for staying in the battle—by trusting the Lord while putting one foot in front of the other.

To Ponder:

What is your definition of courage? How did you arrive at this definition?

What is the most courageous act you have ever witnessed? When have you demonstrated courage?

Why, Lord?

Be strong and courageous. Do not be afraid or discouraged.
1 CHRONICLES 22:13

Shortly after Jay, Holly, and I settled into Colorado Springs, I learned that the buyer for my New York condo had listed the assets she *hoped* to have by the real-estate closing time rather than what she actually had. The deal had fallen through.

Suddenly I was the not-so-proud owner of two mortgages. Meanwhile, war was looming in the Persian Gulf, causing the East Coast housing market to fall. My first job had been for thirty-five cents an hour, so I knew the penny-by-penny value of a dollar. I was terrified at the amount of money I would lose if I was forced to forfeit my down payment on the condo in Colorado Springs.

I spun into almost two months of rereading the Scriptures I felt had lead me to move my family west. I fought my fear that I'd somehow missed God's direction. But the more I read the Word, the more I was reassured God had opened the doors for the move. And I memorized John 16:33 to remind me God said we would have trouble in this world but that he would always be with us.

I further reminded myself I'd made my decision based on the information I'd had at the time, and no amount of hindsight was going to change the way things had turned out. All I could do now was give the situation to God, trust him to bring his good out of it, and stop listening to long-distance "friends" who said maybe I wasn't supposed to have moved, since the New York sale had fallen through. (Why do people do that to us?)

One morning I reached the end of my emotional rope. During my walk, I threw my hands up and said aloud to the Lord, "Okay, I'm done with it. Do what you want."

The first thing God did was to prompt me to feel gratitude for what he *had* given me: a new job, a view of Pike's Peak, two great teenagers. By the time I'd walked home, I was feeling better.

The second thing he did was to lead me to one of the more perplexing stories in Scripture. The morning after my walk, I was randomly thumbing through my Bible—and stopped at Judges 20, the account of the Israelites asking God if they were to fight the Benjamites. Twice he told them to fight. And twice they were soundly defeated—having lost 22,000 men the first day and 18,000 men the second day!

It wasn't until the third battle that he gave victory to the Israelites. Why, I wondered, had God wasted 40,000 men? At least in the book of Job, the reader knows that Job, a righteous man, suffered because of a conversation between Satan and God. But I found no clue in the Judges 20 narrative.

Why did so many men die in battle? Why were the details of my move proving so difficult? I realized that the answer was the same in both cases: God knows. We don't—and this is where walking by blind faith comes in. I had to trust that the Lord was working in my situation, even if I couldn't see the result. And by moving me to a greater spirit of thankfulness, he was opening me to a greater trust in him—whatever the outcome.

By the way, the condo eventually sold—eight months later. Yes, at a loss, but I could handle it then without wringing my hands. It took me a while, but I had finally learned that God would take care of us.

To Ponder:

Have you ever thought you had missed God's will? If so, what was the situation?

Has a financial crunch ever caused you to reexamine your faith?

How do you think we can know when to step out in faith when we don't have a clear sense of God's direction?

Fear of Tripping

*They will lift you up in their hands, so that you
will not strike your foot against a stone.*
PSALM 91:12

A few years ago, sixteen-year-old Holly was convinced our
upcoming move to Colorado would ruin her life. Nothing I
said helped. Then Doug, a friend from our New York church,
told me about one of his experiences working in a physical-
therapy unit:

A man had been under treatment for several weeks, recovering from an accident. The doctors insisted he had no physical
reason for his overly cautious steps, but he ignored their news
that his bones were healed. Then Doug was assigned to him.

Doug watched him take those tiny steps and asked why he
walked like that.

"I'm afraid I'll fall," he answered.

Doug looked at him. "Did you ever fall when you were a
kid?" he asked.

"Oh, sure. Lots of times," the man answered. "My brothers
and I were always chasing each other."

"How about when you were older?" Doug asked. "Did you
ever fall then?"

The man smiled. "Yeah. I played softball. I was always fall-
ing, diving after a ball."

Doug nodded. "Okay, we're going for a walk, and I'm going to trip you. You're going to fall. And you're going to see that it's all right."

The man wasn't sure he could do that, but Doug coached him outside to the hospital lawn. As they walked along, Doug suddenly tripped him, and the man sprawled in the grass.

For a moment, he lay still, mentally checking for broken bones. Everything was okay. He stood up and grinned. Then he bounced up and down and even gave a little jump. He realized he was going to be just fine.

That evening I told Holly the story, then gave her a hug. "So, honey, I'm going to trip you," I said. "But you're going to see that God is leading and that this move will be a good one."

She gave an exasperated sigh, but she knew there was no turning back. And to my great relief, she settled into our new state and new routine with relative ease. Now, years later, she says it was the best move we could have made.

I think of Doug's story whenever I'm arguing with the Lord about another challenge. It seems that just about the time I get comfortable with what I'm doing, he pushes me toward an obstacle that looks as though it will trip me. But what a difference it makes when I choose to see it as an opportunity to grow—and to discover that in him I'm stronger than I think.

To Ponder:

Have you ever known someone like the man who was afraid to fall? If so, how did fear hold that person back from life?

Have your fears ever held you back? When this happens, what do you find helpful?

What advice do you have for those who are afraid to take the necessary steps toward greater freedom?

Tempted by the Easy Way

There is a way that seems right . . .
but in the end it leads to death.
PROVERBS 14:12

Standing for the Lord isn't always easy—as my trip to a southern college proved. The school had been founded on Christian principles but had become lax in its standards over the years. Then a new president came on board, and after a year of studying the situation, including a rapidly declining enrollment, he made the startling announcement that if the college was going to die, it would die Christian!

Next, he told the faculty that if they weren't holding to biblical principles, they could leave. By the time the dust settled—after numerous resignations and firings—he brought in godly teachers who were ready to go down with the academic ship. But the most amazing thing happened: As the school's curriculum, professors, and lifestyle returned to the Lord, enrollment picked up. In fact, within a few years the school had eliminated all debt. Two years later, the enrollment was more than eleven hundred.

When people tried to praise the president for the increased numbers, he shook his head. "No, this was God's work," he said. "After all, he can't bless what will not honor him."

That's a good statement to remember when we're tempted to take the easy way: "God cannot bless what will not honor him."

To Ponder:

When have you been faced with a choice between the easy way and the right way? What happened?

What factors weigh on each side of the decision?

What advice do you have for a young person entering the work world?

Don't Quit Now!

So do not throw away your confidence; it will be richly rewarded. You need to persevere so that when you have done the will of God, you will receive what he has promised.

HEBREWS 10:35-36

The latest article was not going well. I needed fresh ideas, but everything my fingers produced seemed stale. *Ah, Lord, whatever made me think I could write anyway?* seemed to be my most persistent prayer.

Then in the middle of that sluggish Saturday morning, Holly arrived home from college and insisted we go horse-back riding.

"Might as well," I muttered. "I'm not getting anything accomplished here."

Within the hour, we were at our favorite stable, but the docile horse I usually rode was already on the trail for the entire day. There was nothing to do but request the *second* most docile. Soon a large black horse was being led toward me. We eyed each other for a moment, and then I took the reins and led him to the mounting block. There, I placed my left foot in the stirrup and had just started to swing my right leg over the saddle when the horse decided he didn't want me on his back. And he cleverly—and quickly—began to sidestep away from the block. There I was, one foot in the stirrup and

the other poised in midair. Even back then I didn't have the
agility—nor the dainty figure—to shift my weight quickly and
throw myself into the saddle. Instead, I was perched in midair
for a long moment. The stable owner stood below me, arms in
the air as though to catch me when I fell. There was only one
convenient part of my anatomy to push, but he knew me well
enough not to try that. So with arms waving, he hopped from
foot to foot and yelled, "Don't quit *now*, ma'am! Don't quit
now!"

Holly was bent forward in her own saddle, howling with
laughter at the scene, so of course, I started chuckling and
then had an even tougher time hauling myself into position.
But at last, I shoved my foot into the stirrup, the horse gave
a defeated snort, and I turned his head toward the trail.

Right then I knew the ride, even with its tenuous start, was
exactly what I needed to finish my assignment. Besides, I had
too much time and effort already invested in the project to
abandon it. I whispered, "Thank you, Lord," and then, calling
a robust "Don't quit now!" I followed a still-laughing Holly
up the trail.

Whenever I'm tempted to quit in the middle of an
endeavor, I remind myself of that story—and the words of
that stable owner. "Don't quit now!" is a phrase we'd all do
well to remember when times get tough.

To Ponder:

When have you been tempted to abandon a project?
Have you ever been in a situation where no one else could
    put you "in the saddle"?
What advice do you have for others who want to quit?

Learning to Be Strong like Molly Pitcher

She sets about her work vigorously;
her arms are strong for her tasks.
PROVERBS 31:17

Ever have days when you need a reminder that you're stronger than you think you are? When those times hit me, I like to think about the story of Molly Pitcher. You remember her—the colonial woman who carried water to the soldiers in several Revolutionary battles in which her husband fought. Her real name was Molly Ludwig Hays, but as the men called, "Molly! Pitcher!" she gained the nickname that stuck.

During one particularly fierce battle, she saw her husband collapse from heat exhaustion beside the cannon he was firing. She ran to his side, not to cradle him in her arms, but to take his place and fire the cannon!

That's the type of woman I want to be.

As adults of the New Millennium, we often feel as though we're in a battle, too. We worry about bills, the future, our children's education. The list can get rather scary. But worrying doesn't do anything except rob us of physical and emotional energy. If we want to be victorious over all the challenges that surround us, we have to take a deep breath, hang on to the Lord, and grab some of the determination that

Molly Pitcher had. As we stand our spiritual ground and refuse to let problems send us scurrying in fear, we'll be a lot closer to winning our own battles.

To Ponder:

What historical figure do you admire? Why?
Whose example helps you face emotional challenges?
What strengths do you take into your emotional battles?

Courage in Crisis

You, dear children, are from God and have
overcome them, because the one who is in you
is greater than the one who is in the world.
1 JOHN 4:4

Don and I married while we were in college. Two years later, in the middle of my postgraduate work, we began to think about starting our family. At the same time, though, a radical group took over the campus. Every evening, the police arrested another crowd of angry students who had tossed smoke bombs through our lecture-hall windows.

For Don and me, this dangerous activity became more than a political disagreement—it represented everything that could threaten our future children. One Sunday afternoon, I tearfully blurted all this to my mother. She listened, then handed me a tissue.

"I remember being afraid, too," she said. "It was wartime when your dad and I worried about having you. And your uncles were born in the middle of a flu epidemic that was wiping out entire families.

"Your worries aren't new, honey," she continued. "But the Lord brought all of us through those tough times; he'll be with you in whatever you decide, too. Just make sure you're letting *him* rule your life—not fear."

I'm glad I listened to her. After all, I would have missed great blessings if I had allowed fear to keep me from accepting the good gifts waiting for me. Since that Sunday afternoon so many years ago, I've learned (and relearned) that when we start to worry, the only way through the emotional swamp is to concentrate on the Lord's power. And certainly, God's Word is full of stories of people who trusted the Lord through times of turmoil and danger: Deborah, leading her nation during the turbulent era of the judges; King David, battling Israel's enemies; Paul, periodically imprisoned by Rome.

The eternal, all-powerful God is greater than the circumstances around us. Whether we're struggling with a bad day or a national crisis, his strength and faithfulness are more than enough to overcome whatever the world throws our way.

To Ponder:

Have you ever thought about how you would respond if you were placed in a situation where your physical safety was at risk—such as in a crime-ridden neighborhood or a country with civil conflict?

What are your greatest fears for your family? How do you deal with them?

Has anyone ever offered encouragement when you were overcome by fears? What happened as a result?

A Young Mom's Courage

I can do everything through him who gives me strength.
PHILIPPIANS 4:13

Our Tuesday night Lamaze classes were coming to an end. Within a few more weeks, eight little human beings would be kicking the air instead of their mothers' rib cages. As final preparation for our big day, the instructor showed the film of an actual birth.

As we watched the on-screen mother panting at the right moments, each of us thought of our own soon-to-arrive turn on that delivery table. When the instructor turned on the lights, a first-time mother-to-be gasped, "I can't do that!" And she started to sob.

Her emotion was contagious. Suddenly the rest of us had tears in our eyes, too. Then the lone teenager in the room, the one who had her sister as her birth coach, spoke. We knew she had chosen adoption for her baby rather than accept the abortion her boyfriend demanded.

"I get real scared sometimes," she said. "But then I just remember that God's gonna help me. . . . Besides, it's a little late for us to back out of giving birth now."

Several of us chuckled then, and one of the husbands

laughed out loud. Suddenly we relaxed and began to talk about the delivery dates. Within the next month, eight healthy babies arrived despite their first-time-mothers' nervousness.

That brave teen's no-nonsense humor comes to mind as I read Philippians 4:13 with its reminder that we *can* face even seemingly impossible situations in the Lord's strength. Paul declared that, with the Lord as the source of his strength, he had learned to be content whether he possessed much or little. He learned he could do those things God asked because the Lord would give him the necessary power.

Even so many years later, I think of that young woman who encouraged the rest of us. I wonder where she is now, if she's married with other children, and how many times a day she thinks about her first baby. And with each thought of her, I am still encouraged by the memory of her confident "God's gonna help me."

To Ponder:

Have you ever been in a situation where you could do noth-
ing but go forward? What kept you going?
What helps you through challenges today?
What do you wish someone had told you earlier about life's
difficulties?

Lord, I Can't Do This

If any of you lacks wisdom, he should ask God,
who gives generously to all without finding fault,
and it will be given to him.

JAMES 1:5

I'm amazed at how often I've been forced to grow. For example, I had never pumped gasoline before my husband's last extended hospital stay. I ought to be embarrassed to make that confession, but the truth is, I had always been content to have Don take care of that "guy" activity.

The day came, though, when I knew if I didn't fill the tank, I would be stranded on Michigan's expressway. The closest gas station was self-serve only, so I was concerned that I wouldn't pump the gasoline correctly. What if I caused something to jam? Or worse, what if I blew up my end of town because I didn't push the buttons in the right order?

Worried, I pulled into the station and murmured a prayer of "Please help." (I wonder if the Lord ever chuckles at some of our prayers and says, "Believe me, this one is already answered.") As I got out to examine The Pump, I saw to my great relief that the directions were written above the nozzle.

I was studying the directions so carefully that a man who had just finished pumping gas into his own car watched me with a puzzled look. I gave him a wan smile. "I've never pumped gas before," I confessed. "In fact, I'd really appreciate it if you'd watch to make sure I don't blow us all up."

He grinned and then glanced around, probably wondering where the *Candid Camera* equipment was hidden. But he came to stand next to me, offering an encouraging "That's right. Good. You'll be a pro at this in no time."

Well, that little episode proved to be my introduction to the world of auto mechanics, and I even advanced to learning how to change my own oil. But the incident also became a reminder for me not to be afraid to tackle new things.

Pushing beyond our comfort zone to do something new is good for us—it keeps us from becoming emotionally "old," it helps us grow, and—I like to think—it pleases God. After all, the instructions are already there. Besides, how many prayers does he have to field from a gas pump?

To Ponder:

Have you ever been afraid to tackle a new task? What was the result?

What new activities are now part of your routine even though you once were afraid of them?

What advice do you have for others who are timid about trying new things?

TRUST and OBEY

Running to the Mountain

*In the morning, O Lord, you hear my voice; in the morning
I lay my requests before you and wait in expectation.*
PSALM 5:3

After my first year of college, I had stopped off in Kentucky
to visit my grandparents before continuing my bus journey
home to Michigan. Letters from two young men were waiting
for me, both demanding a decision. I didn't want to face any
more challenges, especially as I was still trying to get used to
the absence of Uncle Bob, the Cherokee herbalist who had
always listened to my laments as he sorted roots and leaves
for his medicinal teas. He had died the year before and was
buried in Rest Haven, about a mile up the road from my
grandparents' house.

That first morning there, longing to talk to Uncle Bob, I
grabbed my Bible and ran to the cemetery, through the stone
gates, and up the mountainside to his grave. I sat down next
to his headstone and looked down the valley to the Cumberland River as it meandered past its sycamore-covered banks,
the early morning mist riding on the brown water. The tran-
quillity of the hour was a contrast to the turbulence I felt
inside.

I looked at my Bible, not sure what passage would offer

comfort—or answers for the demands in the letters waiting back at my grandparents' house. I thought of stories I'd heard of others who, looking for solutions to their problems, just opened the Scriptures and found the answer in the first portion they read. So, daring God to encourage me, I opened my Bible to the *Old* Testament—to make sure I didn't hit on Romans 8:28—then with eyes tightly closed, I thrust my index finger onto a page (not a practice I usually recommend). When I opened my eyes, I fully expected to find my hand resting on a list of "begats." Instead, I read Psalm 11:1 (KJV): "In the Lord put I my trust: how say ye to my soul, Flee as a bird to your mountain?"

I gasped. Wasn't that exactly what I had done when I had run to this Harlan County mountain? God hadn't given me specific direction; he was just encouraging me to trust the future to him. And his showing his concern in that precise way would carry me through the days—and years—ahead.

To Ponder:

Have you ever asked God for specific direction? What happened?

Have you ever asked for a particular Scripture? What did you find?

What do you think about asking God for specific guidance?

Real Women Ask Directions

Teach me your way, O Lord; lead me in a straight path.
PSALM 27:11

I like to think of myself as independent, competent, able to cope without help in most situations. But when that independence extends to spiritual self-reliance . . . well, that's another story.

Years ago when I lived in Michigan, I was invited to a special meeting north of New York City. I was elated—and nervous as could be.

New York was the end of the world to me then, and I wondered how I could possibly fly to La Guardia Airport, rent a car, and, even with a map, drive on those mysterious East Coast parkways to the event.

Throughout the flight, I kept running possible scenarios through my head. What if I couldn't figure out the map? What if I got lost? By the time the plane landed and I picked up the rental car, my nervousness had escalated. Before I put the key in the ignition, I leaned my head against the steering wheel and prayed, *Lord, you know I have the worst sense of direction in the world, so please help me.*

Then with a giant sigh, I started out. At each stoplight, I reexamined my map, often whispering, "Which way, Lord?"

Amazingly, at every corner—even the one with the twisted street sign—I turned correctly.

It was an incredible day for me. Not only did the meeting go well, but I, a woman born in the hills of Kentucky, was driving in New York City!

That evening my plane back to Michigan landed at Detroit's Metro Airport right on time. I was a mere twenty-five minutes from home and would drive a route I had driven dozens of times. As I located my car in the parking lot, I didn't *say* it, but my attitude was one of *Thanks, God. Now I'll take it from here.*

An hour later, with my frustration growing by the minute, I was still trying to get onto the main highway, which would take me home. It wasn't until I prayed, again asking for help, that I finally got onto the correct road.

Since that long-ago evening, I've often had to turn my self-reliance over to the Lord, saying, "Please don't let me take it from here." And my dependence on him often starts with the profound one-word prayer: "Help!"

To Ponder:

Has your attitude ever been to take control? What happened?

In what areas are you trying to let God be in control?

How do you help or hinder what God is trying to do? What improvements are you trying to make?

A Gentle Ticking

*This grace was given us in Christ Jesus
before the beginning of time.*
2 TIMOTHY 1:9

One of my favorite childhood memories is of my Kentucky grandparents, Papa and Mama Farley, kneeling by their living-room chairs each evening and praying aloud. I'd try to pray, too, but I was so intrigued by the thought of God's sorting their voices I'd never get through my own requests.

Meanwhile, I could hear the old mantel clock ticking quietly, as it had during the flu epidemic of the early 1900s and World War I. I listened to the same ticking Mama heard in the Great Depression, when she knew the only thing standing between her large family and hunger was the hillside garden. The clock had ticked throughout World War II, when Mama and Papa knelt on behalf of four sons and three sons-in-law stationed in unpronounceable places. And it ticked through the 1950s, when their children moved from their cloistered community to the industrial North.

I think of that little clock whenever the great what-ifs loom: What if something happens to my children or their spouses? What if my health fails and I can't be around for my future grandchildren? What if . . . What if . . .

The Lord doesn't promise we won't have trials—just as Papa and Mama weren't spared all that the little clock ticked through—but we can face problems calmly, knowing God *is* with us.

To Ponder:

What is your favorite childhood memory?

Do you remember a family possession you associate with a happy childhood scene? If so, what is it?

What helps you when the great "what ifs" loom?

Do You Trust Me?

Though he slay me, yet will I hope in him.
JOB 13:15

Whenever I'm struggling with my latest lesson in trusting the Lord, I remember the story of the man who was hiking in the mountains. High above the valley, he slipped and fell. As he went tumbling over slippery granite, he grabbed a sapling growing between two boulders.

"God, help me!" he called.

In answer, a voice from heaven said, "Do you trust me?"

"Yes, I trust you," the frantic man said. "Help me!"

The voice came again. "Do you *really* trust me?"

This time, dangling in midair, the man pondered the question. Finally, he answered slowly, "Yes, I do trust you."

Then the voice came a third time. "Then let go."

Let go? Was there a ledge just two inches below his feet, but hidden from his view? Or was the Lord asking him to abandon himself—and his very life—to God's seeming abyss?

I found myself dangling over an emotional abyss just a couple of weeks before my husband, Don, died. He'd had a rough chemotherapy treatment the day before but insisted I return to my classroom, since substitute teachers were impossible to get for the half-day session before Christmas break. He refused to have a nurse with him, saying he'd spend the morning in his easy chair.

As I dropped our children off at their schools and then hurried toward my own, a new heaviness surrounded me. "Why is this day different, Lord?" I asked.

I gasped at the passage from Job that came to me in response: "Though he slay me, yet will I hope in him."

"Lord, if you take Don, you might as well take me, too," I said. "How will I survive without him?"

I cried all the way to school. I even reminded God of his own Son's prayer, "Father, if you are willing, take this cup from me." But also like his Son, I had to complete that prayer with "yet not my will, but yours be done." And I cried again. (Trusting the Lord doesn't mean our eyes will always be dry.)

Later, I was relieved to see Don smiling at me as I rushed through door after my last class, but I knew our days together were limited. I had no choice but to step into the abyss. But I knew that God would be with me—with us—no matter what the outcome.

To Ponder:

What lessons in trust have you faced? What was the greatest struggle?

Have you ever carried a trust lesson from one situation into the next?

What advice do you have for others who feel as though they are dangling over an emotional abyss?

Angel in Uniform

Whether you turn to the right or to the left, your ears will hear a voice behind you, saying, "This is the way; walk in it."
ISAIAH 30:21

I'm one of those people who never gets on a plane without looking where the emergency doors are. And when I check into a hotel, I locate my floor's exit. Once I've determined my route of escape, I go about my normal, cheerful business.

Jay and Holly have watched me do that since their early childhood, so when we were in Niagara Falls a few years ago, they insisted I change my crisis mode of thinking. I assured them I was only being prepared "just in case." But I gave in to their insistence, and that night in our hotel I didn't look for the stairs nearest our room.

You know what happened, of course. Yep, early the next morning the fire alarm went off. For a startled moment we looked at one another, not believing what we were hearing.

I wanted to yell, "I told you this would happen someday!" But I was the adult, so with seeming John Wayne calmness, I said, "It's okay. Let's just get out of here."

I felt the door, thankful it was cold under my touch. Then I opened it, and we stepped out into a pitch-black hallway. Not even the usual exit lights were visible. I had no idea which way to turn.

"Oh, Father, help us," I implored.

Immediately a woman's voice, with a heavy Hispanic accent, came from the end of the corridor. "Is anyone on this floor?" she called.

"Three of us," I answered.

"Come this way," she said. "Follow my voice."

With Jay and Holly hanging on to my arms, I felt along the wall as we quickly moved toward the woman as she continued to say, "Come this way." At last we could see her in a chambermaid uniform, standing near the stairway.

I thanked her, but she waved toward the steps. "It's okay. But do hurry."

Outside, we moved past the fire trucks to stand with other guests and staff, but we couldn't see our benefactor. Later, we marveled that she had called down the corridor the instant I had prayed for help. We wondered if perhaps heaven hadn't been the scene of an "angel alert!"

We don't always receive such direct, on-the-spot answers to our petitions heavenward, of course. But every now and then, I'm convinced, God *does* intervene directly—or via his messengers. So I keep watching. You never know what form the miraculous will take when it invades the everyday.

Oh, by the way, Jay and Holly have never again teased me about being prepared "just in case."

To Ponder:

What "just in case" preparations do you make?

Have you ever had an immediate answer to a desperate prayer?

What are your thoughts about angels taking human form to help us?

The Pharaoh on the Wall

*But in your hearts set apart Christ as Lord. Always be
prepared to give an answer to everyone who asks you to give
the reason for the hope that you have.*
1 PETER 3:15

While I sat by Don's hospital bed during our battle with his
brain cancer, he liked watching me work on a intricate
needlepoint wall hanging he had asked me to do. He had
dubbed it "The Pharaoh" and had purchased it because of the
Egyptian material I included in my classroom mythology unit.
It had become a family joke, though, as I ripped out almost as
many crooked stitches as I put in. Don already had a spot
picked out in our living room for the prize hanging, so I had
to keep poking the threads through the canvas.

One morning at the hospital, Dr. Nelson stopped by to ask
family medical questions. I opened the canvas bag I carried
constantly and untangled more threads as Don answered.
Occasionally, I corrected him: "Honey, your grandma had
cancer, too. Remember? It was in the 1920s, just after their
visit back to Scotland." Or, "Wait, your brother had kidney
stones a couple of years ago."

Finally, Dr. Nelson turned to me apologetically. "Mrs.
Aldrich, it's important that *Mr.* Aldrich answer these ques-

tions. We need to see how much of his normal brain function has been impaired by the lesions."

Properly chastened, I gave a startled "I'm sorry" and turned back to the pharaoh.

Don chuckled. "But this *is* 'normal brain function' for me," he said. "San's always kept track of the family news. She sends the birthday cards, and at reunions she reminds me which of my cousins are divorced, so I don't ask about the wrong spouse. If you want my family history, you have to talk to her."

I smiled at my bearded Scotsman, grateful for his defense. But I bent over the needlepoint as Dr. Nelson continued the questions. The black border around the pharaoh had given me trouble all summer, so I was anxious to finish it. Then, just as I was ready to connect the sides, I realized I had miscounted the canvas spaces. *Groan.* It would do no good to pull out those hundreds of stitches; much of the background was already completed. My choices were limited. I could abandon this whole project and go back to my quilting, or I could adjust the stitches and accept the slight zigzag that would result.

I glanced at Don as he answered medical questions. How appropriate for me to discover the mistake right then—with him in blue pajamas on top of a white hospital sheet. The needlepoint imperfection was just a tiny reminder of what we were facing in our personal lives. We could give up, saying it was hopeless. Or we could make the necessary adjustments and allow the Lord to create something beautiful out of the imperfect zigzag in our lives. I touched the black broken line in the pattern and spoke to God in my heart. *Create your beauty, Lord. I trust you to bring your good out of this trauma.*

Today, the completed Pharaoh hangs in my home, a reminder that even though God didn't do all we had prayed for, his presence—and beauty—is still with this family.

To Ponder:

How do you react when you're confronted with a zigzag in your life?

How has God brought his good, and even his beauty, out of the zigzags?

Do you have any painful memories (such as a vigil in a hospital room) that you have been able to come to terms with?

Two Faces in the Painting

If you repent, I will restore you that you may serve me.
JEREMIAH 15:19

Several years ago, I had the privilege of seeing Leonardo da Vinci's painting of *The Last Supper* on a monastery wall in Milan, Italy. As I stood before the centuries-old masterpiece, one of the Bible teachers in our group told this story:

Leonardo da Vinci decided to use living models for the thirteen figures in the painting since this scene was such an important aspect of the Lord's life. He started with the face of Jesus and looked all over the area for a young man whose face displayed both celestial beauty and earthly innocence. At last he found him, and the young man sat before him for six months. When the Christ figure was completed, da Vinci then worked for more than six *years* on the other disciples. Only the figure of Judas was left unfinished.

Each day, da Vinci walked the streets looking into the weather-beaten faces of street workers and beggars, searching for someone to portray the man who betrayed Christ. Finally he heard about a prisoner who had been sentenced to die for his brutal crimes. At the jail, da Vinci persuaded the jailer to let him see this hideous criminal. Sure enough, the man's twisted, ugly face was filled with such hate that da Vinci knew he had found the man to represent the one who would betray the Savior.

By special permission, da Vinci arranged to have the prisoner brought to the monastery under special guard to pose. For several months, the man sat before the artist with the guards on either side. At last, the figure was finished, and da Vinci nodded to the guards that they could take their prisoner away. But suddenly the man broke free and rushed to da Vinci.

"Look into my eyes," the prisoner demanded. "Do you not know me?"

The artist looked at the man closely. "No, I do not know you," he answered. "I never saw you before the day I met you at the prison."

As the guards came forward, the man looked heavenward. "Oh, God," he cried. "Have I fallen so low?"

With a desperate look back at da Vinci, he cried, "Look at me again. I was the same man you painted only seven years ago as the figure of Christ."

Of course, we gasped as we heard the story, but then we turned to study the faces of Jesus and Judas more closely. How could the same man have been used as the model for both perfect purity and ultimate evil? As our tour group moved on to another part of the monastery, I turned for one final look at the majestic painting, trusting that I would never take my own spiritual status for granted.

To Ponder:

If da Vinci had chosen you as a model, for which figure in
The Last Supper would you have liked to have been
considered?

Do you know people who, like the prisoner, had their very
countenance altered by life's circumstances?

What is the most interesting part of this account to you?

Caring for the "Unimportant"

And whoever welcomes a little child
like this in my name welcomes me.
MATTHEW 18:5

Several seven- and eight-year-old boys were playing stickball in the dusty street as I came out of my hotel. This was the Middle East, and I was intrigued by the dark-eyed children in their ankle-length blue shirts. I watched them elbow their way to the ball, and a little boy I guessed to be about four came out of a nearby house. He held a stick that was almost as tall as he was, but the "big boys" didn't invite him to play.

Within a few minutes, a man in a long robe came out of the house, touched the child's shoulder, and spoke the Arabic word for son. Happily, the little boy thrust the stick back inside the house and hurried to catch up with his dad.

This is the little boy I see when I read Matthew 18:3-5. In that passage, the disciples had been arguing about who was the greatest in the kingdom of heaven. Each seemed to think he deserved that title. Finally, they decided to let the Lord settle the issue. But instead of naming one of them as the greatest, he drew their attention away from themselves and to a child in the surrounding crowd. He spoke of humility, a lesson the disciples needed to hear. But he also spoke of kindness—kindness to a child, the sort of kindness this Middle Eastern father had shown his son.

It's easy to overlook kids. It's easy to overlook the weak, the unimportant, those who aren't healthy, those who don't look right or haven't achieved much (in our eyes). Even as Christians, we're inclined to admire those who are better dressed, speak well, and appear more "like us."

Jesus doesn't think that way. In his eyes, everyone matters—whether it's a little child or someone who appears small in the eyes of the rest of the world. When we show kindness to the "small people" of the world, we will be rewarded as though we had been kind to the Lord himself.

To Ponder:

Describe the Matthew 18 scene as you see it in your mind. Where do you see yourself?

Do you ever find yourself overlooking the "small people" of the world?

Who are the "small people" in your life to whom you'd like to show more kindness?

Better than a Mule

I will instruct thee and teach thee in the way which thou
shalt go: I will guide thee with mine eye. Be ye not as the
horse, or as the mule, which have no understanding.
PSALM 32:8-9 (KJV)

Whenever I read this passage from Psalm 32, I have two
simultaneous thoughts: I want to be so close to the Lord that
he *can* guide me with his eyes, and I'm determined not to be
like our Kentucky mules, Jack and John.

Those mules were typical of their species with their blue-
black coats and sturdy shoulders that would support the plow
harness for long days in the field. But they were also typical
when, instead of pulling together, they would get ornery and
decide to go their own ways. If they accidentally were placed
in the opposite side of the harness from where they usually
worked, they would fight, even inflicting serious shoulder
bites on each other. And they had a tendency to get spooked
easily.

Once when Dad had only Jack in the plowing harness, he
swatted at a bothersome hornet. Then before Dad knew what
happened, Jack took off toward the road, pulling the plow
behind him. The animal had no understanding that the road
was dangerous, that he could hurt himself, or even that the
man running after him was trying to protect him. Jack, like

all mules, would have run until the plow got tangled up in brush if Dad hadn't finally been able to grab the bit in Jack's tender mouth to stop him.

I don't want to be like our old mule. I don't want to run from the Lord. I want to be so close to him I don't even have to hear his voice but can look directly at him and know what he wants me to do.

When I was growing up, my mother proved it was possible to give guidance with only her eyes. At family gatherings, her expressions could range within a few minutes from "I'm proud of you" to "Don't even think about that" to "Just wait until I get you home!" I want such guidance from the Lord. And it's reassuring to know he has promised to give it.

To Ponder:

Which animal does your most noticeable personality characteristic remind you of?
Which characteristic would you like more of?
How can you develop more of the characteristics you want?

Trusting Those We Love to God

I trust in your unfailing love;
my heart rejoices in your salvation.
PSALM 13:5

Have you ever tried to fix someone else's spiritual life? I have—more than once. But I'm finally learning that all we can do is pray and trust God to work in that person's life. Now as I pray for others, I try to remind myself of a long-ago event that symbolizes what I'm trusting the Lord to do.

When my son was a toddler and his sister just three months old, I had to run some errands. Everything had gone fairly well, even with the baby in my left arm, my purse slung over my shoulder, the purchases in my left hand, and twenty-month-old Jay clutched with my right.

As we approached an escalator, I let go of Jay for just a second to steady myself. Quickly I reached for him, but he stepped back, unsure of getting on anything that moved. The escalator was taking me away as he stood watching. Before I had a chance to panic, though, an older couple walked up behind Jay.

"Please grab his hand," I said. The couple nodded and brought my smiling little boy with them. They were there when I couldn't be.

That's what I'm trusting the Lord for as I pray—that he will supply the right people or the right experiences to grab hold of the person I'm interceding for. And as I pray, I'm remembering the older couple that "just happened" to appear at the precise moment I needed them to rescue my little son. God *does* hear, and he does care. That's what I hang on to when the doubts creep in.

To Ponder:

Have you ever been in a situation in which you had to trust strangers?

Are you trusting the Lord for a particular situation right now?

What's the most difficult part of this situation for you?

I Want Patience—Now!

Therefore, as God's chosen people, holy and dearly loved,
clothe yourselves with compassion, kindness, humility,
gentleness and patience.
COLOSSIANS 3:12

You've probably seen the plaque that says, "Lord, give me patience—now!" And perhaps, like me, you've smiled as you identify with the sentiment. Patience is an area I struggle with because I want things done right—my way—and done *now*. In fact, I've even joked, "Yes, I know God does all things well, but I do wish he was open to suggestions!"

Recently, I was in just such a mind-set as I rushed through Saturday errands, determined to cross a dozen things off my eternal to-do list. At lunchtime I stopped at a fast-food restaurant—and, to my surprise, was soon intrigued by a family with four well-behaved children. Each child had a job: one got the straws, another the napkins, while the oldest brother, all of about eight years old, put the bib around his little sister's neck as she sat in the high chair. Throughout the meal, both the mother and father gently encouraged each child and were patient when one set of little hands slipped on the big cup. I wondered how long it had taken them to develop the loving patience Paul talks about in Colossians 3:12. Undoubtedly, the parents started putting these good habits into practice when the first child was a baby, because it was obvious this wasn't just "for the public" behavior.

As I watched, I thought about Paul's saying that we can choose to "clothe" ourselves with attitudes that include compassion, kindness, and patience. And if we can choose, then we aren't bound by old habits, and we don't have to give in to the pressures—not even endless to-do lists—with an exasperated, hands-on-hips type of attitude.

With that fresh insight, I leaned back and watched the pleasant family scene. As I sipped—and actually enjoyed—my second cup of coffee, I decided to make better choices about the emotional clothing I put on each day.

To Ponder:

Have you witnessed anyone's display of unusual patience lately?

How would you label yourself in the patience area?

What specific improvement would you like to make as you respond to others?

What to Do While You Wait

Find rest, O my soul, in God alone; my hope comes from him.

PSALM 62:5

My husband, Don, and I were getting tired of waiting. We wanted a baby.

The waiting lists to adopt were long. We tried to adopt a little girl and her younger brother who were under the foster care of my Kentucky cousin, but our out-of-state status denied us that. Next we sent no less than twenty-four letters to various organizations in Vietnam, in hopes of adopting a child fathered by an American soldier and abandoned by the Vietnamese mother. We had no way of knowing at the time, but all those letters went across the desk of one American colonel. The man finally took pity on us and wrote to suggest we foster a child through one of several organizations while we waited for the "activity" in that part of the world to be over. More waiting.

Waiting is difficult. Waiting to conceive a baby. Waiting to get on a list for adoption. Waiting to hear about a new job. Waiting to recover from an illness. Waiting for the Lord to reveal a direction and purpose for us. We can feel our life is suspended, on hold.

But while we wait, we still have to live life. God has much to show us. What helped me get through that frustrating time of waiting to be a parent? Even as I struggled with uncertainties of my own, I found that helping others—especially children—did the most to get me through the long days. So with new vigor, I concentrated on my students in the high school classroom, helped with the youth group at church, and wrote letters to the three little girls we had begun to sponsor through a Christian organization.

Most important, I began to concentrate on the Lord's presence in Don's and my everyday lives—instead of demanding he answer my prayers *right now* and in the way we wanted. Gradually, his peace reminded us that no matter what trials we're facing—even if what we're facing is more waiting—his strength becomes ours. And that new understanding alone made the wait bearable.

To Ponder:

What has been the most difficult situation for you to wait through?

What helped you during that time?

What new insight do you hope to take into the next time of waiting?

Our Father's Care

Cast all your anxiety on him because he cares for you.
1 PETER 5:7

The young father in front of me at the mall called out, "Daddy's got ya," as he swooped up the toddler trying to outrun him. The child giggled and then snuggled against his daddy's neck.

I smiled as I watched the scene, then suddenly remembered a long-ago night in our Kentucky farm community. I was five years old, and my parents had taken me "down the road" to visit neighbors. By the time we left their home, the stars were already out, and our lane looked long and dark in the moonlight, especially where the thorny blackberry bushes hung over the ditches. Quickly my dad swooped me up and carried me on his strong shoulders. The night was still dark and the bushes still had thorns, but I felt so safe and warm I fell asleep.

There have been many times in my adult life when I've been carried—by my heavenly Father. And I've noticed that though I long to be carried *away* from the darkness, I'm actually carried *through* it—just as Daniel was saved *in* the lion's den rather than *from* it. I confess, I don't like the challenges and traumas that often come as part of the human existence. In fact, I've even occasionally thought I'd like God to say, "Good morning, Sandra. This is what I plan to do for you today; is that all right?" But, of course, he doesn't, and I'm left to choose whether I will trust him during the scary times.

At one point, I was so intrigued by the word *care* used in 1 Peter 5:7 that I researched it and found that the word is used to convey two meanings—our worry and his comfort. The worrying type of care comes from a Greek word meaning "to divide the mind." And that's exactly what happens: My mind is divided when I allow worries, distractions, and anxieties to interfere with my trust that I'll be swooped up by my heavenly Father and carried over life's dark ditches and past the thorny bushes.

When I do allow myself to rest in him, I can almost hear him whisper, "Daddy's got ya."

To Ponder:

What are the "dark lanes" and "thorny bushes" in your life?

Do you remember a time when you were carried by your heavenly Father?

When have you "carried" another person? What were the circumstances?

The Faces of Angels

See that you do not look down on one of these little ones. For
I tell you that their angels in heaven always see the face of
my Father in heaven.

MATTHEW 18:10

My taxi was caught in the middle of New York City's traffic,
so there was nothing to do but relax. I gawked at the tall
buildings and marveled at the swarms of people on the side-
walk, representing so many nationalities. As my cab inched
forward toward the corner, I could see a little girl standing
alone, fear etched on her round face. People were rushing by,
ignoring her. My thoughts bumped against one another:
That's somebody's little Holly. How can people ignore her?
Lord, protect her. I know, I'll take her to the police station.

Then, just as I leaned forward to tell the driver I'd get out,
a frantic woman darted around the corner, spotted the child
and ran to her, calling her name. When the mother scooped
her up, both sobbed at having found one another.

I breathed a "Thank you, Lord," and settled back against
the taxi seat, thankful he had allowed me to see the rescue.
But I was also saddened by thoughts of the countless situations where the ending is not so happy.

If my pain over that scene as a sinful human was so acute,
then imagine the pain of our perfect heavenly Father over

lost little ones! Of course, I want him to rescue every child himself, but he has left many responsibilities to us. One of those God-given obligations is to care for all children, whether they're born or preborn, toddlers or teens.

Then I thought of my own children who, now grown, were no longer under my daily watchful protection. When they were little, I knew where they were, but now that they're grown, I know only where they're *supposed* to be. *Father, help me to remember that you love my children even more than I do,* I inwardly prayed. *And help me daily to trust them to you.* Sighing, I turned my attention back to the crowds on the sidewalks, marveling that God knows each one by name— and that we parents can trust our children to him.

To Ponder:

What situations cause you to feel powerless?

How do you respond when you see others in trouble? How would you like to respond?

What do you think is a parent's greatest responsibility toward a child?

You Do!

*Call upon me in the day of trouble; I will deliver you,
and you will honor me.*

PSALM 50:15

When Holly was a toddler, her favorite expression was "Me
do!" It didn't matter if she was insisting on pouring her own
cereal, getting dressed, or tying her shoes—she had to be in
charge. Of course, I should have been glad she was determined to be independent, but she wasn't old enough to have
fine-tuned the needed motor skills. Thus, she'd spill the
cereal—hardly my favorite sight when we were in a hurry—put
her little shirt on backward, and get her shoelaces so knotted
I'd have to work a fork prong through the knots to untie them
one by tedious one.

I'll say this for Holly, though. When she had gotten her laces
hopelessly tangled, she'd hand me the shoe and say, *"You do."*

Don't we do the same thing to the Lord? He gives us clear
instructions about life through his Word and wants to lead us
in making good decisions. But no, we get our emotional laces
all in knots. Even then I can imagine God saying, "Give this
to me. Let me help."

That's pretty good encouragement for us to hand our life's
knots to him with a trusting "Here, *you* do."

To Ponder:

What spiritual lesson have you learned from a child?
Have you ever told God, "Me do"? What happened?
Have you ever handed God your "knotted laces"? What was the situation?

Glory in the Darkness

Because of the Lord's great love we are not consumed,
for his compassions never fail. They are new
every morning; great is your faithfulness.
LAMENTATIONS 3:22-23

We three had been in Colorado Springs only a few months, but already things were not going well. The deal to sell our New York condo had fallen through after I had already purchased our new home, the latest storm had damaged the roof, the car's engine developed a short circuit, a surprise bill showed up—well, you get the picture.

I reread the Scriptures I thought had directed our move west. I replayed every event that seemed to point to the rightness of our decision. Still, nothing removed the knot from my chest.

Then one Saturday at 4 A.M., I dropped Jay off at his high school to catch the bus for a regional event. But instead of going home, I drove to a nearby park noted for its majestic red rock formations. I needed to connect with God and be reassured I hadn't missed his voice in this cross-country move—and I thought I could do that best in his world instead of in mine.

As I entered the blackness of the park, I pulled off the narrow road and got out to study the heavens, hoping the beauty of the star-filled sky would offer some encouragement. Suddenly, a bright green meteor shot across the full length of the sky, its brilliance a breathtaking contrast to the darkness around me. Stunned, I said aloud, "Oh! Thank you!" as I watched the trail. As the vivid color faded into the horizon, my problems didn't seem as heavy as before. Oh, they were far from being solved, and I still had to deal with the challenges around me—but I knew that scene would remain with me in the days ahead.

I also knew I would not have seen the Creator's glory without the darkness. Now I would have to take that reminder of his light into my own emotional darkness. As I started the car and headed home, I felt a new sense of peace wrapping itself around me—God's peace.

To Ponder:

What do you do when everything seems to be going wrong? What would you like your reaction to be during those times?

Has the Lord ever stepped into your chaos in a miraculous way? If so, what happened?